THE ALGARVE

TRAVEL AND PROPERTY GUIDE

Brian Nuttall

**Robertson
McCarta**

First published in 1989 by

Robertson McCarta Limited
122 Kings Cross Road
London WC1X 9DS

© Brian Nuttall 1989
© Photographs, Brian Nuttall
© Maps, Kummerly + Frey

Managing Editor Folly Marland
Designed by Bob Vickers and Eric Drewery
Production by Grahame Griffiths
Typeset by Saxon Printing Ltd, Derby
Printed and bound in Italy by Grafedit SPA, Bergamo

This book is sold subject to the condition that it shall not,
by way of trade or otherwise be lent, resold, hired out or
otherwise circulated without the publisher's prior consent
in any form of binding or cover other than that in which it
is published and without a similar condition including this
condition being imposed on the subsequent purchaser.

British Library Cataloguing in Publication Data

Nuttall, Brian
    The Algarve travel and property guide.–(The travel
    and property guides)
    1. Portugal. Algarve. Visitors guides
    1. Title II. Series
    914.69'6'04427
    ISBN 1-85365-177-X

Every care has been taken to ensure that all the information
in this book is accurate. The publishers cannot accept any
responsibility for any errors that may appear or their
consequences.

CONTENTS

CONTENTS

CONTENTS

PREFACE

The Algarve has emerged as a major European holiday and tourist region in the last twenty five years. It has grown particularly rapidly in the last ten years. I made my first visit in 1969 to Monte Gordo for a family holiday, returning in 1972 to buy a house at Carvoeiro. Since then hardly a year has passed without a visit, usually several. Much has changed during that period.

About two years ago I tried to find a detailed guide book in the bookstores of Faro and Portimão. There were many on Portugal but none of any depth on the Algarve, which has, historically and geographically, for centuries been considered as a separate kingdom, albeit within Portugal.

Hence this book, which has two main functions. First, it sets out to provide information for those who are interested in the region in some degree of detail in travel guide format. Secondly, it aims to provide information and advice on the ever expanding property market, where to buy, relative to your requirements and purse, and the pitfalls to avoid.

Acknowledgements

A large number of people have assisted me during the research for this book and to whom I offer my thanks for their time and trouble.

The Portuguese National Tourist Office in London and the Algarve Tourist Board gave much information for which I am indebted.

Many estate agents were most helpful but in particular, Roger Willcock of Urbinvest, Vilamoura, who helped me unravel that complex development. Brian Pullin of Vilas and Homes, Jose Santos of Seleccao Imobiliaria, John Griffiths of Griffiths & Griffiths of Lagos, John Garveigh of Alpart, Lagos and many others who assisted with invaluable property information.

On the technical side I would like to thank David Sampson, Solicitor, for providing detailed information on the legal processes, Denis le Mare, an established resident, for his valuable advice and Richard Wall of Deloitte Haskins & Sells, Lisbon, for his clarification of the complicated and changing taxation system.

Tony Barnabe, the professional at Vilamoura Golf Club and a member of the Algarve Tourist Board, kindly helped with the section on sport, particularly on the location of the planned new golf courses.

I trust that I have achieved the intended objectives and that it will give you, the reader, as much pleasure as it gave me, the author.

Brian J Nuttall FRICS   July 1989.

Estrada de tráfico internacional Carretera de tráfico internacional Route de transit international Internationale Fernstrasse International throughroute	Capital regional Capital de región Capitale régionale Regionalhauptort Capital of region **Faro**	Outras curiosidades Otras curiosidades Autres curiosités Andere Sehenswürdigkeiten Other objects of interest ★
Estrada camarária Carretera de tráfico regional Route de transit régional Regionale Fernstrasse Regional throughroute	Parque natural Parque natural Zone de protection naturelle Naturpark Natur area	Miradouro Vista panorámica Point de vue / Aussichtspunkt View point ☆
Estrada de ligação principal Carretera de comunicación principal Route de communication principale Hauptverbindungsstrasse Main connecting road	Localidade de veraneio Localidad de veraneo Station de villégiature estivale Sommerferienort Summer holiday resort Carvoeiro	Torre / Farol Torre / Farol Tour / Phare Turm / Leuchtturm Tower / Lighthouse
Estrada de ligação Carretera de comunicación Route de communication Verbindungsstrasse Connecting road	Estação de férias aberta todo o ano Localidad de vacaciones durante todo el año Station de vacances pendant toute l'année Ferienort während des ganzen Jahres Holiday resort throughout the year Albufeira	Aeroporto / Aeródromo Aeropuerto / Aerodromo Aéroport / Aérodrome Flughafen / Flugplatz Airport / Airfield
Outras estradas Otras carreteras Autres routes Übrige Strassen Other roads	Catedral, igreja, capela Catedral, iglesia, capilla Cathédrale, église, chapelle Kathedrale, Kirche, Kapelle Cathedral, church, chapel	Motel; pousada Motel; posada, parador Môtel; pousada, parador Motel; Pousada, Parador Motel; pousada, parador
Caminho, atalho Sendero, camino de herradura Sentier, chemin muletier Fussweg, Saumpfad Footpath, mule track	Santuário, mosteiro Santuario, monasterio Eglise de pélerinage, couvent Wallfahrtskirche, Kloster Pilgrimage church, monastery	Hotel isolado Hotel aislado Hôtel isolé Alleinstehendes Hotel Isolated hotel
Estrada macadame ou em mau estado Carretera no revestida o en mal estado Route sans revêtement ou en mauvais état Strasse ohne Belag oder in schlechtem Zustand Unmetalled road or road in bad condition	Castelo Castillo Château Schloss, Burg Castle	Praia / Termas Playa / Balneario Plage / Station thermale Strandbad / Heilbad Beach / Spa
Trajecto pitoresco Recorrido pintoresco Parcours pittoresque Malerische Wegstrecke Scenic road	Palacio Palacio Palais Palast Palace	Parque de campismo de temporada Camping de temporada Camping saisonnier Saisoncampingplatz Seasonal camping
Ferry-boat Transbordador Bac pour automobiles Autofähre Car ferry	Ruína (idade média) Ruina (edad Media) Ruine (moyen Age) Ruine (Mittelalter) Ruin (medieval)	Parque de campismo aberto todo o ano Camping abierto todo el año Camping permanent Ganzjähriger Campingplatz Camping throughout the year
E14 **92** Numeração das estradas Numeración de carreteras Numérotage des routes Strassennumerierung Road numbering	Monumento romano Antigüedad romana Monument romain Römisches Baudenkmal Roman antiquity	Fronteira Pasaje frontera Passage frontière Grenzübergang Frontier crossing
Distâncias em quilómetros Distancias en kilómetros Distances en kilomètres Distanzen in Kilometern Distances in kilometres	Monumento Monumento Monument Denkmal Monument	
Caminho de ferro Ferrocarril Chemin de fer Eisenbahn Railway	Forte Fuerte Fort Fort Fort	
Fronteira nacional Límite de Nación Frontière d'Etat Staatsgrenze State frontier	Caverna, gruta Caverna, gruta Caverne, grotte Höhle, Grotte Cave, grotto	
Limite regional Limite regional Frontière régionale Regionalgrenze Regional boundary	Museu Museo Musée Museum Museum	

1:200 000

0	5	10	15	20 km
0		5		10 miles

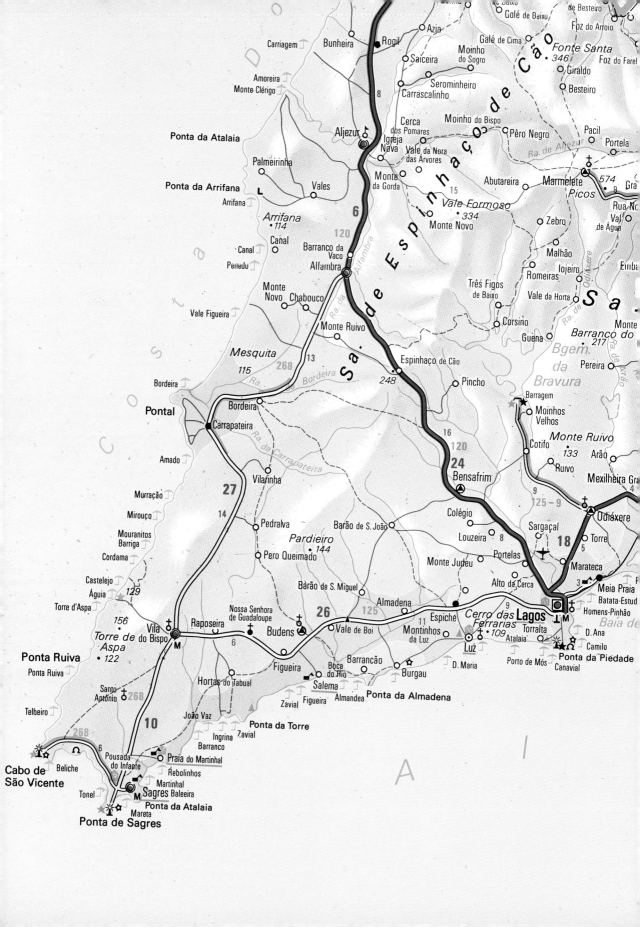

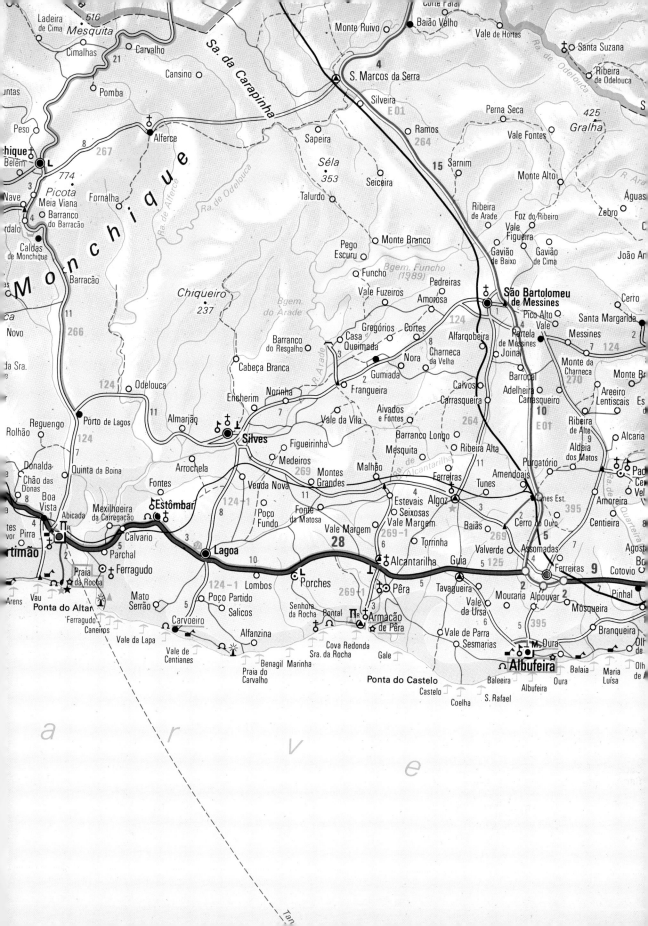

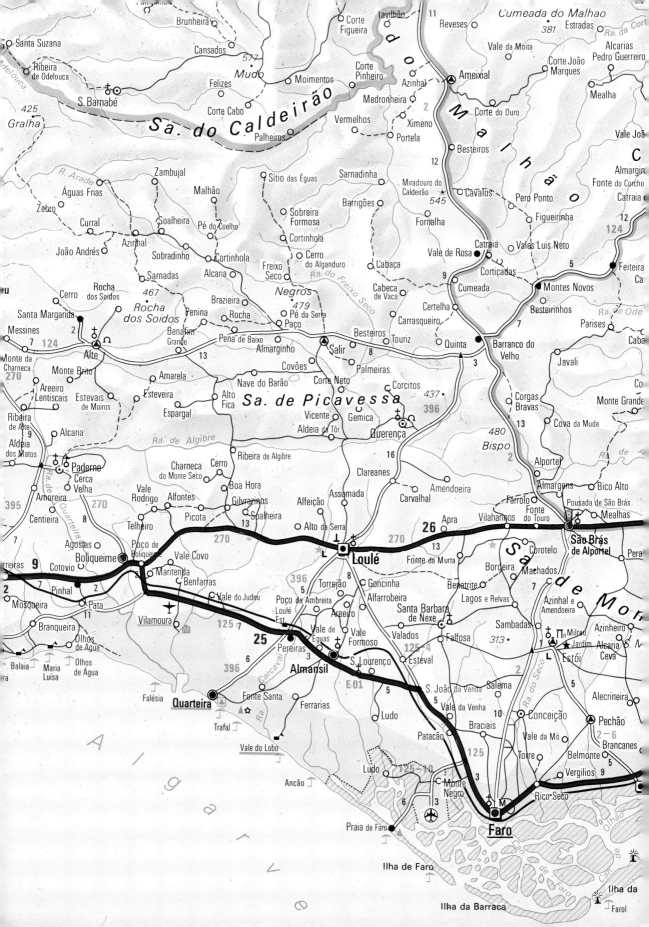

PART I

BACKGROUND AND PRACTICAL INFORMATION

History

Prior to the Roman occupation, very little hard fact is available about the history of the Algarve. In the western part of the Iberian Peninsular, the Ligurians, people who lived near what is now Genoa, intermarried with the Celtiberians: a mixture of the Celts from northern Europe and aborigines called Iberians. The resulting amalgam was the Lusitanians, considered to be the original natives of Portugal, although their territories then spread into what is now Spain. Lusitanos is a term used with pride by the present day Portuguese.

The Phoenicians, Carthaginians and Greeks all traded along the coast between 1000 BC and 500 BC but the Roman legions' arrival in 218 BC during the Second Punic War, began their occupation, which lasted about six hundred years. The occupation was not without problems; the Lusitanian War lasted twenty years and later uprisings were led by Viriathus, later honoured in literature and art, and Sertorius, but subdued finally by Caesar and Augustus between 61 and 15 BC. The Roman province of Hispano Ulterior is divided into Baetica (Andalusia) and Lusitania, the latter being of only marginal importance to the Romans. The basic road system laid down by the Romans exists today as do the fish salting beds and, more recently discovered, the remains at Vilamoura, Milreu and Ossonoba (now Faro).

The Vandals and Visigoths followed in the early part of the 4th century AD, the latter adopting the Roman Catholic faith and persecuting Jews. In 711 AD the Arabs (Moors) defeated Roderick, the last Visigoth King and controlled the whole Iberian Peninsular, although their main influence was in the south where they established a base at Xelb (Silves).

The Moors controlled the Algarve, which then extended further north, covering the southern half of Portugal, until the middle of the thirteenth century, giving it its name *Al-Gharb*, meaning the occident or west. The Moors were a mixture of tribes, not united and many

Roman mosaic, Cerro da Vila, Vilamoura

came from the Yemen. The Islam faith dominated although Christianity and Judaism were tolerated and it is believed that the Old Testament was the first printed work in Portugal.

The Moors' influence and heritage is enormous in many spheres, not least in agriculture and food. The almond, orange and carrot were introduced by the Moors as indeed was their technique for extracting olive oil and sugar. In language many words begin with the prefix *al-*, as in *aldeia* (village), *alcofa* (basket) and towns such as Albufeira, Algoz and Alvôr. In literature and the arts their influence was strong. Ibne Asside, born in Silves, an astrologer, philosopher and lecturer was highly regarded in his time along with Ibne Caci, ruler of Mertola and Silves, a theologian and ascetic. Culture and poetry flourished, particularly in Silves.

The Moors lost Silves briefly in 1189 when Dom Sancho I captured it, only to lose it again in 1191. It remained under the Moors until 1249 when Dom Alfonso III with the Knights of St James, led by Paio Peres Correia, took both Silves and Faro. This brought the Moors' resistance to an end.

The Algarve entered a period of peace whilst the frontier with Castile was confirmed on the River Guadiana, a treaty of friendship was signed with England and King Joao I, as head of the House of Avis, had a major victory over Castille at Aljubarrota. This confirmed Portugal's independence and João's reign saw the beginning of colonial activities and the voyages of discovery which were to establish Portugal as a leading maritime nation.

In 1415 the important trading post of Ceuta in Morocco was captured by the Infante Dom Henrique, son of King João I and Philippa of Lancaster, thus grandson of John of Gaunt. He was knighted by his father and made Duke of Viseu.

From about 1418 Henry set up a simple lifestyle in the western Algarve, possibly near Raposeira, but he was attracted to Sagres, where his ambitions to spread Christianity, and enlarge the Portuguese empire took root. Supported by his father and the Pope, he gathered cartographers, mathematicians, navigators and sailors about him which resulted in the major voyages of discovery which continued after his death in 1460, and well into the sixteenth century. Madeira, the Azores and Cabo Verde islands were discovered where negro slave trade began and only ended in 1850. The renowned sailor Gil Eanes eventually rounded Cape Bojador in Africa in 1434, Bartolomeu Dias rounded Cape of Good Hope and Columbus reached the West Indies in 1488. Vasco da Gama discovered the route to India in 1498 while Cabral reached Brazil in 1500. This brought worldwide trade and prosperity to Portugal during the reign of D. Manuel I (1495-1521), making Lisbon a focal point. Magellan rounded the southern tip of South America and, despite his assassination in the Philippines, one of his ships completed the first circumnavigation of the globe in 1522. This was perhaps a fitting tribute to Henry without whose initial enthusiasm and impetus, the voyages would not have taken place, although ironically, he never personally sailed beyond the north west coast of Africa.

The early and mid-sixteenth century saw a decline in fortunes under King João III. Following the successive deaths of Sebastião I (1578) at the disastrous battle of Alcácer Quibir, and Henrique II (1580), the House of Avis and Portugal's independence came to an end, as Philip II of Spain, a grandson of Manuel I, overran the whole country.

Little occurred to disturb the Algarve during the period of the Spanish domination, except perhaps the British expeditions which burnt Faro in 1596. This occupation lasted until 1640, when the Duke of Braganza, related to the old royal family, restored independence by leading a successful uprising in Lisbon and was crowned King João IV (1640-56). In 1654 a treaty of friendship and commercial co-operation with Britain ensured independence from Spain but at the same time set up a British predominance for the future, further enhanced when Catherine of Braganza, sister of King Alfonso VI (1656-67), married Charles II of Britain.

The reign of José I (1750-77) was called the age of *absolutism* during which the Marquis de Pombal had much influence in the fields of manufacturing, trading, finance, law and education. It was the same Pombal who directed the rebuilding of Lisbon after the great earthquake of 1755 which also caused great devastation in the Algarve.

In 1807 the Napoleonic armies gained the right to march through Spain as a result of the Treaty of Fontainebleau and General Junot invaded and occupied Portugal. The royal family fled to Brazil and it was not until 1811 that Portugal was liberated from the French after Wellesley (later Duke of Wellington) and British troops repelled first Junot and later Napoleon's own forces. Uprisings in the Algarve, particularly at Olhão made a significant contribution in the eventual freedom.

The next hundred years, until 1910, passed relatively quietly for the Algarve, although various revolutions, new constitutions, new political parties and dictators occurred in the seat of power to the north. The country's financial situation became critical, slowly undermining the monarchy, until King Carlos and his heir were assassinated in 1908. Carlos's younger son Manuel II was unable to save the monarchy and fled to Britain as the Republic was founded in 1910.

Throughout the two world wars Portugal remained neutral. Salazár became Prime Minister in 1932 and ran a Fascist dictatorship, solving the long standing financial crisis, but causing isolation amongst western countries following the Second World War until his retirement on health grounds in 1968. His more liberal successor Caetano was brought down in the 'Carnation Revolution', an almost bloodless army-inspired coup of 25 April 1974. My own presence in the Algarve at that time witnessed little more than extensive grafitti, billposting and the closure of Faro airport for three or four days.

But the most far reaching influence upon life in the Algarve, indeed in its long history had already happened. Tourism had arrived the previous decade. It was now to receive a severe check as a result of the 1974 Revolution; the world energy crisis; high unemployment; rabid inflation; half a million refugees from Mozambique and Angola, a general unrest and the flight of capital.

Financial collapse was averted by help from the European Community and other countries, and a democratic parliamentary republic was established in 1976. Tourism in the Algarve recovered slowly in the late seventies but a succession of coalitions and caretaker governments continued until 1987, when for the first time since the 1974 revolution, one political party, the Social Democrats, achieved a working majority.

Tourism is now the lifeblood of the Algarve and thus dependent upon the prosperity of other European nations, primarily its oldest ally Britain. Now a member of the European Economic Community, Portugal has much to gain from its entry.

Culture

THE PEOPLE From the total Portuguese population of about ten million, 300,000 live in the Algarve in an area of approximately 2,000 square miles. This is, however, an increasing figure as tourism attracts more people from the north and indeed other nationalities, who arrive for employment and prosperity, quite apart from the climate and quality of life.

By nature, the Algarvian characteristics are similar in many respects to the fishing folk of other regions. The way of life has traditionally been hard and produces resilient, courageous people. It is, however, the Moors who have had the greatest influence upon the Algarvian character. The Moors themselves, a mixture of races united by their belief in Allah, occupied an area about a half of modern Portugal as well as large areas of southern Spain. To them the Algarve was a kind of paradise; a favourite place and they said and wrote beautiful words about it. After the conquest of the Moors, many remained, predominantly Yemenites, some of whom were converted to Christianity while others became hostages or slaves. Today that element is still prominent, mixed through intermarriage with different ethnic races. It is evident in facial features, inclinations and in the abilities of the true Algarvio. He has been said to have "the fatalism, the superstitions, and presentiments of the Arab, a man of order and peace. His heart is great. His dignity greater. And a wound to his pride can put him into a blind rage. Possibly his greatest defect is egotism, as with all men".[1]

The great period of sea voyages, exploration and colonisation has also left its mark upon the character of the Algarvio. The origin of this wanderlust is ingrained in the personality of Portuguese men and it has had an impact on the economy of the country, causing a shortage of skilled labour and a type of 'brain drain'.

Instant impressions of calm dignity, spontaneous friendship and generosity will soon become evident to anyone who meets and mixes with the Algarvians.

THE ARTS Apart from a few sites and ruins, such as those at Milreu and Vilamoura, there are few antiquities from Roman or prehistoric times. From the eleventh century onwards, just before independence, art and architecture assumed a national character.

Romanesque architecture arrived during the eleventh century with the Burgundian knights from France. Gothic styles developed at the end of the fourteenth century. However, few examples have survived the earthquake of 1755, except perhaps the castles and city walls built as a defence against the Moors and latterly the Spanish.

The Manueline style is a transition from the Gothic to Renaissance and is named after King Manuel I. Despite its brief duration (1490-1520), it is quite distinctive and original and reflects the age of discovery, sea voyages and the riches thus accumulated. The twisted rope-like column is its typical feature but nautical cable or mariners' knots were often used carved as decorative adornments. Sculpture

---

1. *Terra Morena* by Cesar dos Santos

of the same period expressed the style in window and door decoration comprising laurel leaves, roses, acorns, ropes, anchors and globes. The Cross of the Order of Christ appears regularly. Manueline painters (1505-1550) created their own school which had a realism in composition, was delicate in design and accurate in colour.

The Renaissance retained its French and Italian characteristics and there are several fine examples in the Algarve.

The Classical period of the seventeenth century brought churches with a rectangular plan and without transept, and painting came under the Spanish influence.

The Baroque style (late seventeenth to eighteenth century), whose name derives from *barroco* meaning 'a rough pearl', abandoned Classical symmetry, accentuated curved lines and sought grandeur, coinciding with the end of Spanish domination. Elaborately carved woodwork, often for altars and usually gilded, became the main adornment as well as wood carved statues on the altarpieces.

Azulejos – clay, glazed, decorated tiles – were introduced by the Moors and were first made in Portugal in 1584. These tiles were originally blue, hence the name, from *azul.* The seventeenth century brought mastery of the technique and the introduction of other colours. In the mid-seventeenth century, public buildings were decorated with azulejos depicting pictures or scenes, although later, during the Baroque period, they became used more for frames or settings. Mass production began in 1767 when the Royal Pottery was set up.

Literature in Portugal grew with the birth of the nation and first examples are from twelfth and thirteenth centuries when Kings D. Sancho I and D. Dinis I and their courts, wrote poetry in song format. Throughout, the poetry has shown characteristics of melancholia, nationalism and criticism of the times. Little of consequence occurred during the fourteenth and fifteenth centuries but the Renaissance and the voyages of discovery gave impetus and royal patronage to both prose and poetry. Ribeiro, author of the novel *Child and Damsel*; Ferreira who wrote *Lusitanian Poems;* the famed Luis Vaz de Camões, considered to be Portugal's greatest writer, who wrote the epic *The Lusiads*, a retrace of the voyage of Vasco da Gama, all made significant contributions.

The seventeenth century, during Spanish domination, was unremarkable, but literature in the eighteenth century was revived through literary societies and when Bocage, of French descent, wrote some fine lyrical and satirical poetry.

Monchique parish church

The nineteenth century brought Romanticism, due primarily to Almeida Garret who was not only a poet, but a novelist and playwright. Contemporary authors of influence include Pessoa and Régio, the latter introducing a 'modern movement'. Recent literature, since the revolution of 1974, has had a tendency toward more liberal and socialist expressions.

In the eighteenth and nineteenth centuries Portuguese music was dominated by opera but in the Algarve two folk dances, the *corridinho* and the *baile mandado,* which appear to originate from Scotland and brought over in the nineteenth century, are still evident today. The former is a swift swirling dance and the latter more unusual as the couples form a circle and move to the singer, rather like a square dance. Both are used as tourist attractions.

Fado, a melancholic song form, probably originated from Lisbon but can be heard in the Algarve. It expresses loneliness, nostalgia and passionate emotional feelings. An interesting experience but not if you are in need of 'cheering up'!

TRADITION, FOLK ART AND THE ALGARVE HOUSE

The music and dance referred to earlier are part of the tradition of the Algarve but the religious and public festivals play a major part. These are listed under Part IV Leisure (page 105). These festivals allow the visitor to see the traditional costumes, rarely seen on other occasions.

True folk work takes you away from the tourist locations, usually inland. Esparto, a light fibre, is woven and twisted into baskets, mats and hats, sometimes dyed or interwoven with wool. Basketry is made in two main areas: the Monchique hills as far as Silves and the Guadiana valley. Wickerwork technique does not alter from other parts of the country but the styles and shapes vary. Monchique baskets are a darker brown whereas from Odeleite or Vila Real they are made from osier or willow and used to carry or catch fish.

The Monchique region makes fine decorated blankets and lace and crochet are common, made by the women to supplement the income from fishing. Loulé is a centre where excellent examples can be found.

Earthenware pottery is abundant and often tourist orientated, but there are several genuine new potters, particularly around Porches, where a visit will show work using traditional designs and new ideas.

Chasing of copper is carried out in Faro and Lagos, the latter producing the fine *cataplanas* used for cooking the traditional clams and pork dish.

The Algarve traditional house is squat, single storey, plastered and

Azulejos, church of San Lourenco

whitewashed, and only the frames around doors and windows make a contrast with colour. In the central and eastern Algarve the roof tiles are replaced by an *açoteias* or terrace, particularly at Olhão and Fuzeta. Occasionally in Tavira and Santa Luzia the terrace is replaced by a four sided low pitched roof.

The *platibanda*, later referred to as 'roof decorated walls', is one of the most attractive and distinctive features. It is simply a panel or wall hiding the roof itself. Luz and Tavira provide many lovely examples.

Finally, the Algarve chimney is of course renowned. It is delicate, slender and individual and quite different to the big Alentejo chimney. It is the chimney and the roof decorated walls that are the unique features that distinguish the Algarve house from the rest of the country. The modern Algarve house has held on to some of the traditions, particularly colour and general shape, but density and over development in some locations has attracted deserved criticism which will be touched on later in this book.

FOOD AND WINE

Fish predominates along this coastline with shellfish of all types – tuna, sardines, mullet, bream, swordfish, sole and cod in plenty. *Caldeirada*, a fish stew with potatoes and tomatoes is a local speciality while *Bacalhau a Bráz*, salted cod cooked with fried potato and onion is unusual. Meat is plentiful, pork being most common, and beef and ham, the latter usually smoked. Roast kid, suckling pig rabbit and game are to be found inland. *Cataplana*, the name of the sealed copper dish, is a traditional seasoned casserole for clams, ham and sausage. Inland in the hills, *Cozidos*, again a type of stew, contains cabbage, chick peas, beans, pork, raw bacon and sausage.

The well irrigated valleys produce some fine fresh vegetables and much is also now grown under plastic greenhouses. Soups made from vegetables include Caldo Verde, potato and cabbage, and Gazpacho from tomato, garlic, pepper, marjoram and olive oil.

Desserts are perhaps less interesting, the almond dominating both cakes and tarts. Chocolate Mousse and Creme Caramel are common but the *Dom Rodrigo* and *Morgado* are traditional delicacies, again almond based.

The wines of the Algarve are not rated that highly amongst Portuguese wines. Wines, however, from all over Portugal are available in restaurants and shops and at very modest prices.

The district of Lagoa, where there is a wine co-operative in the town which can be visited, is perhaps the best Algarve wine

House in Tavira

producing area. White, red and rosé are produced, with a white aperitif type having a 16 per cent alcohol content. Portimão and Lagos are smaller but quality producers, while Tavira also produces good wines from the Fuseta and Moncarapacho country. The co-operative system of collection and production applies in these regions also. *Medronho* is a spirit produced in the Monchique and Espinha de Cão mountains. This mixture of brandy and honey results in a very strong sweet liquor. Beware!

Landscape and Climate

The three thousand square miles of the Algarve is open to the south, protected from the heat of Africa by the sea and screened from cold northerly winds by the mountain ranges of Serras de Monchique and Caldeirão. These factors dictate the climate which is Mediterranean in character having hot summers, mild winters and low rainfall.

Physically the high mountain region or *Serra Algarvia* is a schist, not a hard rock but cut by rivers and streams that flow east, south and west. Here the vegetation is cork and holm oaks, rock roses, some terraced cultivation near water and eucalyptus where nothing else can survive.

Lower down, a calcareous zone stretches east to west beneath the hills and is known as the Barrocal, where trees are low, rocks project and fig, almond and carob abound. This is followed by the flat, well watered coastal plains reaching to the sea and known as the Litoral. Here alluvium soils allow groves of fruit trees and vegetables, but vineyards, fig and almond where there is less water.

Vertically, the Algarve has traditionally been divided into the Sotavento (the sheltered side) and the Barlavento (the side from which the wind blows). This division takes place roughly at Albufeira where long sandy beaches give way to cliff beaches. Thus the western Algarve has a cooler, windier more maritime climate and the east a warmer, drier environment. There are degrees of variation between the two general divisions.

The Algarve claims one of the most equable climates in Europe with winter temperatures rarely falling below 15C (60F) and summer temperatures ranging from 20C (68F) to 28C (85F). Rainfall is moderate in the winter (10-20") and low in summer (5"+) but there are over 3,000 hours of sunshine — a very high proportion compared with other resort locations.

FLORA AND FAUNA

Beneath the high point of the hills, trees dominate the landscape, particularly in the Monchique area. Cork oak, olive, pine, eucalyptus, chestnut and willow by the streams abound. Lower in the Barrocal where limestone rock outcrops, carob, olives, gorse and broom grow with wild iris, gladioli and orchid.

Between the foothills and the coast, almond trees are in profusion and the white blossom, anytime from late January to early March depending on the weather, is a magnificent sight. Olives, carob and fig are seen interspersed with potatoes, cereals and other vegetables. Nearer the coast, with more water available, citrus and vineyards take precedence and huge plastic greenhouses are everywhere along the tourist coastline, providing tomatoes, strawberries and vegetables. Hibiscus and bougainvillea provide some spectacular colour in summer while cane and bamboo line the banks of streams. Wild flowers to be found include crocus, orchids, lily, bluebell and sea daffodil.

The virtually treeless area to the west of Lagos has a more Atlantic climate than the rest of the Algarve but is nevertheless interesting with wild iris, antirrhinum and narcissus very common.

The fox and wolf have become rare and the badger even more so. The rabbit is more common than the hare, which is found in the cultivated lower areas. *Cobras* is the Portuguese word for all non-poisonous snakes and should not cause alarm. The only poisonous snake is the *vibora* or 'snub nosed viper' found only in dry rocky locations. Harmless lizards up to eighteen inches long, geckos and salamanders are quite common especially in high summer.

Wild beach flower

The Algarve is a birdwatcher's paradise offering a huge variety of sea, marsh and land birds. The list is endless but some of the more striking are the long crested long-billed hoopoe, the white stork which nests on church belfries and notably on top of the Arch in Faro's city walls, eagles, vultures, kestrels and game such as partridge in the hills. The cliffs of the Barlavento have ravens, jackdaws, gulls and choughs while the marshes, particularly the Ria Formosa nature reserve and the Alvôr estuary have a wide selection of waders, herons and wildfowl.

ECONOMY

Once dependent upon fishing and agriculture, the economy of the Algarve is now based firmly upon tourism. Fishing is still very important with the canning of sardine and tuna for export making a valuable contribution. Fruit and vegetables are grown for local consumption but olives and tomatoes are exported mainly to the United Kingdom. Cork from the cork oak tree is important, Portugal being the world's largest producer of cork.

Portugal's recent entry into the EEC is having, and will continue to have, a major influence on the Algarve and Portugal's economy. Already the benefits are in evidence as new roads and bridges, dams and reservoirs are planned and constructed. Portugal and the Algarve have everything to gain from the membership.

Tourism has had a significant impact in the last twenty years and has in fact altered the character of the Algarve. Development associated with this industry has been criticised but now a master plan for the Algarve is being prepared and will be published in 1990, meanwhile controls have been tightened. Tourism has brought employment, prosperity and foreign investment but also a dependence on the success of other European economies, primarily Britain. This is now changing as other nationalities, German, Belgian, Dutch, and Scandinavians are being attracted to the Algarve in larger numbers.

POLITICS

Portugal became a republic in 1910 but party disputes prevented radical reforms, particularly land reform. Little was achieved by the new system and the 1920s saw much unrest, uprisings and the formation of a communist party. In 1930 Salazar founded the National Union, a Fascist party with a one party state ideal and became Prime Minister in 1932.

The next thirty-six years were effectively a dictatorship under Salazar, who initially solved the economic crisis that had crippled the country for decades, and introduced a new constitution that prohibited strikes and abolished trade unions. A treaty with Spain, renewal of the alliance with Britain, agreements with the USA and other NATO countries to have military bases in the Azores, did not ultimately prevent isolation due to Salazar's authoritarian regime and colonial policy. Membership of the United Nations in 1955 later brought severe condemnation from that same body, over the policies and unrest, particularly in Mozambique and Angola. In the Sixties serious inflation set in due to these colonial wars and Portugal's misguided membership of EFTA.

In 1968 Salazar retired on grounds of ill-health and was succeeded by Caetano, a colleague whose more liberal policies were opposed mainly by the army. Portuguese Guinea declared its independence and finally the dictatorship was overthrown by the army in the virtually bloodless 'Carnation Revolution' on 25 April 1974.

With inflation running at 35 per cent, unemployment aggravated by the return of troops and refugees from the colonies at 15 per cent; a world energy crisis; a series of coalitions and further attempted coups, did not help the cause of putting Portugal on its feet. It was not until 1987 that one party was able to command a majority, when Cavaco Silva, an Algarvio from Boliqueime, led the Social Democratic party to victory.

Present policies include de-nationalisation of banks and insurance companies but inflation is still not under control and runs at an admitted 12 per cent (April 1989). Foreign investment is encouraged and the EEC membership should ultimately assist.

The new constitution of 25 April 1976 was amended in 1982 and the military Council of the Revolution abolished. The constitution was to be upheld by a Constitutional Tribunal of civilian judges elected by parliament. Parliament took responsibility for the military and its role was redefined to 'ensure the defence of the Portuguese republic'.

The head of state is the President who is elected for five years. The parliament, the Assembly of the Republic, is elected for four years and has 254 members. The President can dissolve it but not during its first six months or the last six months of his own office. The President appoints the leader of the government following the verdict of the polls.

Portugal is divided into historical provinces and administrative districts of which the Algarve is one and the same, but for administration purposes is called Faro, run by a Civil Governor based in the City of Faro. Districts are further sub-divided into councils *(concelhos)*, urban and rural.

Portugal is a member of the United Nations, NATO, the Council of Europe, OECD, EFTA, and the EEC.

Practical information

HEALTH

The standards of health care are not as high as in Britain or other more sophisticated European countries. There is a reciprocal health arrangement between Britain and Portugal and some other countries. If however, a prolonged stay or permanent residence is contemplated, private medical insurance is advisable.

The main hospitals are at Faro and Portimão but there are several smaller hospitals and a number of private clinics as well as the British Hospital in Lisbon. The following list should be helpful:

Faro Hospital: Tel: 089 22011/2
Albufeira Hospital: Tel: 089 52133
Olhao Hospital: Tel: 089 72055
Tavira Hospital: Tel: 081 22133
Lagoa Hospital: Tel: 082 52102
Lagos Hospital: Tel: 082 63679
Loule Hospital: Tel: 089 62013
Vila Real de Santo Antonio Hospital: Tel: 081 43166
Clinica Pé da Cruz, Faro: Tel: 089 20102
Clinica do Carmo, Faro: Tel: 089 28352/29226/29665
Medico-Dental Clinic, Vale Formoso, Almancil: Tel: 089 95453
(Dr Andrew French - Paul Tortz (Dentist).
Portimão Hospital: Tel: 082 22132
Portimão: Policlinica, Praia da Rocha. Tel: 082 27842
Clinica de Lagoa: Tel: 082 52749
Carvoeiro Branch: Tel: 082 57741
Monte Carvoeiro (Dr Peter Pertl) Tel: 082 57720
Plaininveste, Praia da Luz: Tel: 082 69866/69811/62891
Faro: Dentist (Dutch) Henri Godefroy Tel: 089 813483
British Hospital in Lisbon Tel: 01 6022020/603786

Water: it should be noted that tap water is considered safe to drink in almost all areas of the Algarve but this is not common practice, especially by non-residents and bottled mineral water is readily available.

Chemists *(Farmacia)* are open 9.00am-1.00pm and 3.00pm-7.00pm Monday to Friday and 9.00am-1.00pm Saturday. Each town has one open for after hours emergency service.

TOURIST INFORMATION

There is a network of Tourist Information Offices throughout the Algarve operated by the Algarve Tourist Region whose head office is

Faro. The Portuguese State Tourism Department in Lisbon can also provide information. Their addresses are as follows:

Algarve Tourist Region
Rua Ataide Oliveira, 100
8000 FARO
Tel: 089 24067-26049 Telex: 56578

Portuguese State Tourism Department
Avenida Antonio Augusto de Alguiar, 86
1000 LISBON
Tel: 01 575015 Telex: 13408

LOCATION OF TOURIST INFORMATION OFFICES

Albufeira
Rua 5 Outubro Tel: 089 55428/52144
Aljezur
Largo do Mercado Tel: 082 72229
Armação de Pêra
Avenida Marginal. Tel: 082 32145
Carvoeiro
Largo da Praia do Carvoeiro. Tel: 082 57328
Faro
Rua da Misericordia, 8-12 Tel: 089 25404/24607
Lagos
Largo do Marquês de Pombal. Tel: 082 63031
Loulé
Edificio do Castelo. Tel: 089 63900
Monte Gordo
Avenida Marginal. Tel: 081 44495
Olhão
Largo 1° Dezembro. Tel: 082 22065/23695
Praia da Rocha
Rua Tomas Cabreira. Tel: 082 22290
Quarteira
Avenida Infante Sagres. Tel: 089 32217
Silves
Rua 25th April. Tel: 082 42255
Tavira
Praça da Republica. Tel: 081 22511

INFORMATION AVAILABLE

Each Tourist Information Office provides a leaflet on the town and locality, giving a street map, an area map, information on local history, handicrafts and traditions, as well as sites of interest to visit.

Beaches and suggested excursions are also covered. These are most useful for instant, brief details and are updated regularly.

MUSEUMS, ARCHAEOLOGICAL SITES, CHURCHES

Museums are usually open between 10am and 5pm, some closing for an hour or two for lunch. Archaeological sites are open for similar periods with some reduced hours in winter months.

Churches are more often than not closed except the more popular such as Faro Cathedral, which has hours similar to those mentioned above. However, access to churches can usually be obtained from a nearby caretaker or keyholder and enquiries at a local cafe or bar will invariably produce a result.

The following is a very brief summary of the principal attractions, which are detailed later, working west to east:

Sagres Fortress and Cape St Vincent.
Lagos City walls churches and museum.
Silves castle and cathedral.
Loulé castle, museum and churches.
Archaeological sites at Vilamoura and Estoi.
São Lourenço church, Almancil.
Faro Old City, cathedral churches and museums.
Tavira castle and churches.
Castro Marim castles churches and museums.

Faro Cathedral

BANKS AND CURRENCY

The government is in the process of de-nationalising the banks and recently the hours of opening have changed. Banks now open from 8.30am until 2.45pm and most do not close for lunch.

The currency is the *Escudo* represented by a $ sign after the sum and acting as a decimal point in the event of there being *Centavos*, of which there are 100 to the escudo.

Banks offer two types of account to foreigners – a Tourist account or Residents account – the latter only being possible when a *Residencia* has been obtained which then entitles you to an interest bearing account. Tourist accounts do not attract interest. It is a criminal offence to write a cheque without sufficient funds to cover it and the matter is reported to the Bank of Portugal and the police. Overdrafts are not available and loans for specific periods difficult to obtain, particularly at the time of writing (May 1989) when the government has tightened lending restrictions in an attempt to curb inflation which is running at 12 per cent or more. Mortgages are also very difficult to obtain from Portuguese banks but can be obtained through off-shore sources and are referred to in Part II of this book.

The principal notes are 100, 500, 1000, and 5000 escudos and coins for the lower denominations. Travellers cheques are widely accepted in banks, hotels, shops and restaurants and there is a small commission charge. Eurocheques supported by a Eurocheque card are becoming more accepted and these can be arranged through your own bank.

Credit cards are also more and more acceptable not only in hotels, restaurants and shops but also to obtain cash. Access, Visa, American Express and Diners Club are the more common but garages rarely accept credit cards for the purchase of petrol, so have cash available when travelling.

PUBLIC HOLIDAYS AND FESTIVALS

Every town has its own local holiday and usually others often associated with a patron saint. Festivals are all about music, song, eating and drinking and these are referred to in more detail in Part IV.

The official Public Holidays are as follows:

1 January (New Years Day)
25 April (Revolution Day)
1 May (May Day)
Corpus Christi - variable.
10 June (Camões Day - the poet)
15 August (Assumption)
5 October (Republic Day)
1 November (All Saints Day)
1 December (Independence Day)
8 December (Immaculate Conception)
25 December (Christmas Day)

25 April celebrates the *Carnation Revolution* in 1974. May Day is a traditional European holiday. 10 June celebrates Camões, Portugal's finest and most famous writer. The remainder are religious days apart from 5 October which refers to the founding of the Republic in 1910 and Independence Day relates to independence from Spanish domination.

SUNDRY INFORMATION

Shopping

Shops are open from 9.00am to 1.00pm and from 3.00pm to 7.00pm from Monday to Friday and are closed on Saturday afternoon and all day Sunday. There are, however, exceptions to this general rule and several supermarkets and other essential goods shops are often open on Sunday.

The traditional shopping centres are in the main towns of Faro, Portimão, Lagos, Loule, Albufeira, Tavira and Vila Real, roughly in order of importance and facilities. Pedestrian shopping areas are available in most of these towns and covered markets, selling a wide variety of goods apart from the usual fresh fish, fruit and vegetables, are in all main towns and many smaller ones.

Port wine and very drinkable white, red and rosé wines are competitively priced. Leisure wear is very good quality and value while copper, basketwork, crystal glass, leather shoes and bags are excellent buys.

The Media

Newspapers from other countries arrive a day late and are available from newsagents and bookshops in towns or from hotel foyer bookstalls. Locally-produced English language magazines include *Algarve Gazette*, *Discover* (divided into areas and also published in German), *Algarve Magazine* and *Algarve News*. These are all monthly publications except *Algarve News* which is published every two weeks and is more of a newspaper than the others. The *Gazette*, *Discover* and *Magazine* are basically advertising mediums, heavily reliant on the property market but nevertheless do provide interesting feature articles and local current information on events, restaurants, sport and other topics useful to both tourist and resident.

Portuguese television has two channels and shows a lot of English language films and series with sub-titles. However, the satellite revolution has begun, with dishes appearing everywhere. Now a variety of channels can be obtained from all over Europe including BBC and this is mentioned in more detail in the Appendix.

At the time of writing commercial radio licences were due to be allocated to support national radio, whereas until recently anyone could open a commercial station, now made illegal.

Postal and Telephone services

The Portuguese postal service is not the most efficient. Recent increases mean a letter within Portugal requires a 29 Esc stamp and may take between one and three days to reach its destination. Within Europe a 60 Esc stamp is required and you should allow at least a week for delivery. Efficiency is improved if you are a resident or there on a regular basis by having an Apartado or Box number, especially if you live some distance from a Post Office.

Post Offices are open from 8.30am to 6.00pm, closed on Saturday and Sunday and some close for lunch in the smaller towns.

CTT, *(Correios e Telecomunicacôes)*, operate both the telephone and postal service in Portugal, the former improving with the installation of new equipment at exchanges, but is still one of the most frustrating features of life in the Algarve. Continuously engaged lines, particularly to some areas like Portimão area or Vilamoura are commonplace. Often a call to Britain is easier to connect than a local call. Area codes are mentioned throughout this book but often the code is omitted from an advertisement or card for some strange reason. For the sake of clarity they are as follows:

Faro area 089 (As far west as Albufeira and almost to Tavira)
Tavira 081 (Tavira to the the Spanish border - Guadiana)
Portimão 082 (West of Albuferia to the Cape and north)
Lisbon 01

Some International codes:
United Kingdom 00 44 France 00 33 West Germany 00 49
Ireland 00 353 Norway 00 47 Sweden 00 46

Remember if the local code within the country begins with a '0', do not dial this digit.

Time relative to GMT

On the last Sunday in March the clocks are put one hour forward ahead of Greenwich Mean Time. On the last Sunday in October the clocks are put one hour back.

Electricity

Voltage is normally 220 volts AC with continental two pin plugs. Thus most UK appliances will work provided the plug is changed, or an adaptor, readily available, is used.

Getting to The Algarve

INFORMATION

Tourist Information Offices are available in the following European Capitals and in North and South America:-

Belgium, Holland and Luxembourg
50, Rue Ravenstein, 1000 Brussels, Belgium.
Tel: 02 5132736/5110880 Telex: 26531 CTP B
Javastraat, 96-2de Verdiep, 2585 A.V. Den Haag, Holland.
Tel: 070 639358 Telex: 34592 CTP NL

France and Italy
7, Rue Scribe, 75009 Paris, France.
Tel: 1 47425557/47425321/47425981 Telex: 220550
Piazziale de Agostini, 3, 20146 Milano, Italy.
Tel: 02 470659-4223214 Telex: 321280 FEXPOR

Great Britain and Ireland
New Bond Street House, 1/5 New Bond Street, London W1Y ONP
Tel: 01 493 3873 Telex: 265653 PORTUG G
Portuguese Embassy, Knocksinna House, Knocksinna, Fox Rock
Dublin 18, Republic of Ireland. Tel: 894416 Telex: 30777

Spain
Gran Via, 27-1, 28013 Madrid. Tel: 34-1 2224408/2229354
Telex: 27283 CTP E
Ronda de San Pedro, 7-1, 08010 Barcelona Tel: 3177999
Calle Marques de Valladares, 29-31 Vigo Tel: 224959

Sweden, Denmark, Iceland, Norway and Finland
Linnegatan,2, S 1147 Stockholm, Sweden.
Tel: 46-8 602654/602613/600108 Telex: 17414 CTP S
Norre Voldgade, 9 1 SAL, DK 1358 Copenhagen K, Denmark.
Tel: 131200

United States, Canada and Brazil
548 Fifth Avenue, New York, N.Y. 10036-5089
Tel: 212 3544403/6/7 Telex: 234140 CTPA UR
1801 McGill College Avenue, Suite 1150, Montreal P.Q. H3A2N4
Canada. Tel: 514 282 1264/5/6 Telex: 05-267312
Avenida Paulista 2001, 16 andar, Conj.1603, Caixa Postal
22045 -CEP-01311, Sao Paolo, Brasil. Tel: 55-11 2888657/744
Telex: 011 21371 ICEP BR

West Germany, Switzerland and Austria
Kaisserstrasse, 66-4, 6000 Frankfurt/M, Bundesrepublik,
Germany. Tel: 49-69 234094/7 Telex: 413976 CTPA D
50, Quai Gustave Ador, 1207 Geneva, Switzerland.
Tel: 022 357410 Telex: 27709 ICEP CH

PASSPORTS AND VISA REQUIREMENTS

Nationals of most countries need only a passport to enter Portugal. Visas are not required for stays of up to 60 days, after which an extension may be obtained from the Foreign Registration Service.

OVERSEAS CONSULATES IN THE ALGARVE

Austrian Consulate
Rua Cãetano Feu, 2 - Praia da Rocha, 8500 Portimão.
Tel: 082 25041 Telex: 57337
Consul: Hugo Stumpf.
Office hours 10.00-12.00 - 14.00-18.00

German Consulate
Avenida da Republica, 166, 8000 Faro.
Tel: 089 22050 Telex: 56515
Consul: Enzio von Baselli und Sussenberg.
Office hours: 9.00-12.00 - 14.00-18.00

Italian Consulate
Rua 25 de April, 65, 8900 Vila Real de Santo Antonio.
Tel: 081 44274/43053
Consul: Luigi Gian Baptista Rolla
Office hours: 9.00-12.00 - 14.00-18.00

Icelandic and Swedish Consulates
Rua Judice Biker, 11, Apartado 105, 8502 Portimão.
Tel: 082 82135 Telex: 57637
Office hours: 10.00-13.00 - 14.00-18.00.

Dutch Consulate
Rua Frei Lourenço de Santa Maria, 2-1, 8000 Faro.
Tel: 089 20903
Consul: João Pinto Dias Pires.

French Consulate
c/o Lusotur SARL - Vilamoura, 8125 Quarteira.
Tel: 089 33033 Telex: 56894
Consul: José C. da Cunha Motta.

Finnish Consulate
Rio Seco, Vale d'el Rei, 8000 Faro
Tel: 089 25482 Telex: 56560
Consul: Pertti Mikko Pohjaniema
Office hours: Daily.

Spanish Consulate
Rua Duarte Pacheco, 21, Apartado 90, 8900 Vila Real de San
Antonio. Tel: 081 44888
Consul: Joaquin Rodriguez Menendez
Office hours: 8.00-13.00 - 14.00-18.00.

Danish Consulate
Praça Visconde Bivar, 4, 8500 Portimão
Tel: 082 23131/2 Telex: 57390
Consul: Alberto Cardosa Ribeiro Azevedo.
Office hours: 10.00-12.00 - 14.00-16.00

British Consulate
Rua Santa Isabel, 21-1, 8500 Portimão.
Tel: 082 23071/27057
Consul: José Manuel Pearce de Azevedo
Office hours: 9.30-12.30 - 14.30-17.00.

Belgian Consulate
Rua Conselheiro Bivar, 10-1 Dto, 8000 Faro.
Tel: 089 27119 Fax: 27164
Consul: João Manuel Baptista Maximiano
Office hours: 10.00-12.00 - 15.00-18.00.

CUSTOMS REGULATIONS AND CURRENCY

Visitors can take in personal effects and holiday equipment without the payment of duty and there are the normal duty free allowances within the EEC rules for the importation of tobacco, wines and spirits. A modest amount of currency may be taken in and out of the country (50,000 Esc. going out and no more than equivalent of 100,000 Esc.in other currency) but large amounts require special permission through the Bank of Portugal and/or the Foreign Investment Institute (see Part II). Check with your bank on current currency regulations which are subject to frequent change or with the Portuguese Chamber of Commerce and Industry (see Appendix).

There is no limit on the use of credit cards or traveller's cheques issued outside Portugal but visitors entering must have a minimum of 10,000 Esc. and 2,000 Esc, or equivalent currency, for each day of intended stay.

HEALTH REGULATIONS Vaccinations are not required for visitors from Britain and most European countries unless there is a current epidemic. Vaccination Certificates are required against cholera and smallpox for those travelling from countries where there are epidemics. Medical insurance is always advisable and in the UK a DHSS leaflet SA30 (which encloses a CMI form) and resulting E111 certificate must be produced for treatment of emergency cases, which is usually free.

AIR

Scheduled services. (TAP and European carriers)
The following services are available:

TAP Air Portugal operate direct to Faro from London (Heathrow) and also to Lisbon with connecting flights.

British Airways operate from both London (Heathrow and Gatwick) and Birmingham direct to Faro, and also to Lisbon with connecting flights.

Dan Air operate a scheduled service to Lisbon where a connecting flight can be taken.
(See Appendix for useful telephone numbers).

Charter Operators. (UK and European)
Seats are available on charter flights from many UK and European cities. The Tourist offices issue a Tour Operators' Guide listing flight and package operators, which contains over 150 companies. This is a changing and volatile market and your travel agent or newspaper will give you the up-to-date position.

Faro airport is building a new, larger terminal building which is due for opening in 1989 which should improve the present over-crowded facilities. Other airstrips exist at Vilamoura and at Alvôr, near Portimão, where light aircraft can operate, although the latter has recently extended the runway and larger aircraft can now land and a service is planned to and from Lisbon.

ROAD AND SEA Foreign registered cars may enter Portugal for up to six months on production of the registration document and 'Green Card' insurance. British and most other nationality driving licences are valid for six months. Cars not registered in the driver's name should have a letter of authority from the owner.

There are numerous Cross Channel services between England and France all available direct or from travel agents. The driving distance to Faro is approximately 1,400 miles and Lisbon 1,200 miles.

There is a car ferry from Plymouth to Santander in northern Spain operated by Brittany Ferries (Tel: 0752 21321), which takes about 24 hours. Driving distances from Santander are about 800 miles to the Algarve and 600 miles to Lisbon.

Frontier posts are usually open from 7.00am to midnight, some closing earlier in winter and some open 24 hours in summer. Check with your tourist office.

Road approaches and routes from the north and Spain will be provided by the motoring organisations but the obvious and direct border crossings are at Caya/Badajoz (Spain)-Caia/Elvas (Portugal) and Ayamonte (Spain)-Vila Real de Santo Antonio (Portugal) via a ferry across the River Guadiana. This latter option will be replaced by the new bridge, upstream, currently under construction and due to be opened in 1991. Two other crossing points at Rosal de la Frontera (Spain)-Vila Verde de Ficalho, which is on the Seville to Beja road and at Valencia de Alcantara (Spain)-Marvão (where there is a Pousada) on the Caçares to Lisbon road, are other options but less direct.

HARBOUR AND MARINA FACILITIES

Seafarers have a choice of harbours along the Algarve coastline. The main marina with comprehensive facilities is at Vilamoura which has over 1,000 berths with power and water supplies, accommodation, restaurants and the Nautical Club.

Vilamoura Marina, 8125 Quarteira. Tel: 089 32023 Telex: 56843

Other anchorage and harbour facilities include Faro, Lagos, Portimão, Olhão, Sagres, and Vila Real de Santo Antonio.

The appropriate reference books are the Admiralty Publication 1972 NP67, *West coast of Spain* and *Portugal Pilot* and *Roteiro da Costa Algarvia* edited by the Hydrographic Institute.

RAIL

Not the most practical or comfortable mode of transport to the Algarve, but possible. There is a daily service from London (Victoria) via Paris across Spain to Lisbon which takes about 25 hours. 'The Sud Express' between Paris and Lisbon has first and second class carriages, restaurant car and sleepers. Other European capitals can connect with this service in Paris.

From Lisbon (Barreiro) a service will take you on to the Algarve and Faro in about six hours. The main rail line between Vila Real de Santo Antonio and Lagos provides a local service along the coastline and roughly follows the line of the main EN125 road but often the stations are some distance from the town which they serve.

Travel in the Algarve

ROAD Generally the rules of the road are similar to other European countries, driving on the right and overtaking on the left with priority for traffic approaching from the right and for pedestrians on zebra crossings.

Speed limits are 60kph (37mph) in towns, with trailers 50kph (31mph); on main roads 90kph (55mph), with trailers 70kph (43mph); and on motorways a minimum speed of 50kph (31mph) and a maximum of 120kph (75mph). Seat belts are required to be worn by drivers and front seat passengers, except in towns.

Car hire operators require a valid driving licence and the minimum age for hire is 21 years for small cars, 25 years for larger cars. Drivers are required to have held a licence for a minimum of one year.

Petrol is sold in litres (approximately 4.5 litres to the gallon) and is available in two grades, Super (4 star) and Normal (2 star). The carrying of petrol in cans is forbidden. Credit cards are not commonly accepted at garages although this is changing.

The main east to west road, the EN125 is generally in good condition the majority of it being single carriageway but some new sections are wider or part dual carriageway. It is subject to steady improvement and currently a much needed by-pass is being built round Almancil, due for opening during 1989. Other roads vary in condition but inland and north of the EN125 are usually good. Between the EN125 and the coast the roads receive the most traffic and consequently are often in bad condition, made worse in the areas of intense development where they are often dug up to connect services. Potholes recur regularly because they are inadequately repaired and maintained. Much criticism has brought some improvement and promises. However, major roadworks and civil engineering projects are in hand which should dramatically improve the Algarve road system. The new bridge over the River Guadiana is under construction north of Castro Marim and will link with a new motorway standard road which will run north of the EN125, initially to Guia (north of Albufeira) but ultimately on to Lagos. The final route is not yet certain and there is a reluctance to make information available despite earlier assurances on this very important subject.

Both the bridge and the road known as the *Via Infante* are planned to be completed by 1992, the bridge which will also link to the EN125 hopefully a year earlier. A new bridge is also under construction to eventually carry the new road across the River Arade at Portimão on to Lagos. This is upstream from the existing narrow bridge which causes enormous traffic congestion in and around the town, especially in high summer.

A few words of warning are appropriate here about driving standards. Currently, Portugal has the worst road accident record in the EEC and driving standards are candidly unacceptable. Driving too close to the vehicle ahead, overtaking on blind bends and brows of hills are commonplace offences. The majority of Portuguese are first generation drivers and the young therefore lack experience as passengers. I believe that the Arab heritage with its endemic lack of regard for human life, is responsible for much of the appalling driving, frequently evidenced by the clear lack of awareness of danger. So beware and take care!

RAIL

Main East-West line

This line runs between Lagos and Vila Real de Santo Antonio and takes over five hours from end to end, most trains stopping at most stations. It is an interesting way to see the Algarve as it follows the coast from Vila Real to Faro then moving inland and returning to the coast near Lagos. Tunes is the junction north of Albufeira which connects to Lisbon.

Lisbon line

This line joins the East-West line at Tunes and takes about three or four hours to Lisbon (Barreiro) from Tunes, some trains being non-stop. There are five or six trains per day in each direction. Fares are low but comfort is not a priority!

BUS AND COACH

Rodoviaria National provides frequent coach services between all main centres as well as to and from Lisbon in about five hours. Timetables can be obtained from local Tourist Offices or travel agents.

TAXIS

Available widely and recognisable by black livery with green roofs. Not expensive but many do not have meters and they are significantly more expensive in the Algarve than in Lisbon.

For a list of guides see the Appendix in Part VII.

PART II

INVESTMENT IN THE ALGARVE

The opportunity for investment in the Algarve falls broadly into two categories: property and business. I will deal with them in that order but first let us look at the political climate and conditions which prevail and make Portugal attractive to foreign investors.

As a result of the election in 1987 the political situation has become stable for the first time since the revolution of 1974. A single political party has a working majority and can implement policies without hindrance or reliance on a coalition party.

Portugal joined the EEC in January 1986 as a full member and in addition has a special relationship with EFTA countries, providing duty free trading with these markets.

Foreign investment is actively encouraged and supported by government policy and incentive schemes are available for appropriate projects. Perhaps the most important factor is a pleasant social environment and an equable climate in which to live and work.

Purchase of property

The growth of the tourist industry in the Algarve accelerated rapidly with the opening of Faro airport. Property purchase by foreign investors increased alongside until the revolution of 1974, when the market virtually collapsed and did not recover until 1978/9. The last ten years have seen enormous growth in the construction of residential property, some of which has been well planned but some has been uncontrolled and excessive in density. Demand, apart from the immediate post-revolution years, has been high, particularly from the United Kingdom where a prospering economy has provided funds for individuals to invest in overseas property.

GENERAL PRINCIPLES The broad principles of buying property anywhere apply but there are some special factors. Location – distance from the airport, transport and shops, sports and leisure facilities — are all important. Estate agents in Portugal are licensed by the government and you should only deal or negotiate through such agents. If you are buying from a developer, check out his reputation and his financial standing as far as possible. Consider whether the contract is fair and straight forward and if you have any guarantees for the money you are paying, relative to the building progress. Check if you have a firm completion date and if you can retain money against any faults in the building work or against late completion.

Letting the property can provide a good income and cover running costs. Consider if it is located in an area that will make it easy to let and what it might realise on an annual basis. In general terms the further west away from the airport or inland away from the coast, the lower the rental value. Properties on a complex with facilities command higher rentals as do houses with private pools but there may be restrictions imposed by the developers. Check carefully the rules of the complex, relative to letting and guests' use of facilities.

Management of the property in your absence is vital. On a complex the developer may well provide this facility and you should check on the cost of management, what it includes, look for any hidden costs, and legally demand a budget of the current year. If you are purchasing an individual or second hand property you should consider who will manage it for you and you may deem it appropriate to have an existing property surveyed. There are not many surveyors at present conducting this type of work but some are listed in the Appendix.

FINANCE   There are two golden rules!

- Do not sign a binding contract for purchase until you have finance arranged.
- Do not commit yourself to a purchase unless you are satisfied that you can afford the capital sum and the outgoings.

Letting a property and treating it as an investment can assist financing but do not expect to let the property for the whole season.
There are two main ways to finance a property purchase :

1. Cash and bank loans. Loans can be arranged through stock banks against various forms of security including bonds, stocks and shares, National Savings Certificates and endowment policies. The most common method to date has been to borrow against the unused equity in the purchaser's main residence.
2. A loan against the security of your Portuguese property is the other option. This is difficult as Portuguese lenders are not as yet actively making loans to foreign investors. Foreign banks are not allowed to take a mortgage charge over property within Portugal.

It is possible, however, to purchase a property through an off-shore company, usually based in the Channel Islands or Gibraltar and raise a mortgage of up to 70 per cent. The shares in the company are held by the lender as security and the company is administered by trustees in Gibraltar or the Channel Islands. This method is gaining in popularity particularly due to the fact that when the property is ultimately resold, the shares in the company are transferred to the new owner thus avoiding the SISA (10 per cent) or purchase tax and the usual conveyancing costs in Portugal

THE LEGAL PROCEDURE

If professional advice can be obtained in respect of value or the quality of the building it should be sought at an early stage. Some developers and agents seek reservation deposits which may or may not be returnable. The legality of this procedure is doubtful and it should be resisted whenever possible.

Instruct a lawyer to act on your behalf who will then carry out searches to check ownership, title, description of the property, mortgages, charges and any other interests.

THE PROMISSORY CONTRACT FOR PURCHASE AND SALE

This is the vital binding document signed by both parties. It sets out the terms of the transfer, the price and time involved and any other relevant conditions. It is essential that all terms agreed are itemised as it cannot be altered after signature.

A deposit will be required upon signature of the contract and may vary from 10 per cent to 50 per cent of the price. Thirty per cent should be the maximum deposit and should not be paid over until the vendor's title has been thoroughly checked. Deposits are often not refundable and should you require this condition then it should be a term of the contract or you should obtain a receipt from the agent of the vendor.

The contract must have a closing or completion date and in the case of building land a backstop date of two years is usually inserted which if not complied with allows the vendor to buy back at the original price. Planning delays are now on the increase since restrictions have tightened.

Failure to comply with conditions will result in the purchaser losing his deposit or the vendor having to repay double any monies received. Good legal advice is important particularly where part ownership or timeshare is involved. The contract ideally should be signed by both parties in front of the local Notary but this is often dispensed with, especially when purchasing from a reputable developer. When purchasing from a private individual it is advisable.

It is also wise to obtain a translation of the contract.

A Habitation Certificate is required and is issued by the local authority (Camara) after inspection to ensure that it has been constructed in accordance with the planning consent and building regulations. Completion, the Deed of Transfer or 'Escritura' cannot be effected until this is presented to the Notary, unless the property was built before 1951. Nothing can be moved into the property until this document has been obtained.

EXCHANGE CONTROL

To effect completion of your purchase you will require a licence from the Bank of Portugal to import the funds for the purchase price and any other monies required. The application may be made by the vendor, his agent or your own lawyer. The procedure can take up to four months and the Bank now check all prices. The Bank of Portugal will not give consent if the value put forward is below the value for the SISA (property tax).

Should your purchase include agricultural land then confirmation from the Ministry of Agriculture is also required that the land is not part of an agricultural reserve before the Bank of Portugal will grant a licence. The Bank will not grant a licence for land in excess of 5,000 square metres of agricultural land without consent from the Foreign Investment Institute.

With the Bank of Portugal licence obtained for purchase, a licence to export the capital upon sale will be granted.

COMPLETION OF PURCHASE

The *Escritura* or deed of purchase is prepared and signed before a notary by you or your representative and the vendor. At the same time the balance of the purchase price is paid over.

If, however you have bought on a development, most of the funds may well have been paid over in stages and it is certainly advisable not to pass over the total amount until the final deed has been execcuted. Twenty-five per cent would be a sensible amount to retain.

An alternative is to place the funds in an Escrow account and these are not released to the developer until all conditions have been met.

LAND REGISTRY

The last stage is for the notarised *Escritura* to be lodged at the local Land Registry in your name. It is also necessary to register the transfer at the local tax office. It is most important that the land is properly identified and that any possible rights of way are checked out by the lawyer.

TAXATION AND COST OF PURCHASE

SISA, a transfer tax or Stamp Duty is payable by the purchaser at the rate of 10 per cent of the price on urbanized land and at 8 per cent on rustic land. There is, however, an annually renewable exemption on residential property, but not land where the price is less than 10 million escudos. The SISA is paid before the signature of the *Escritura* before the Notary. Furthermore the local tax office can challenge the recorded price if they consider it too low.

Traditionally low values have been declared for SISA purposes but the system has now been tightened and it is not advisable to under-declare.

CONTRIBUTION PREDIAL OR REAL ESTATE TAX

A major reform of the Portuguese tax system is in hand and discussed later in this section, but this tax is now charged on all property annually by the local council. It is at a rate of between 1.1-1.3 per cent and charged on the rateable value of the property as assessed by the local council. This is applicable from 1st January 1989 but any changes should be checked with a lawyer or accountant as this tax is under severe criticism.

The Notary and Land Registry fees together are approximately 2.5 per cent of the purchase price.

Your own lawyer's fees will again be a percentage of the purchase price and can be agreed in advance.

SERVICES

The connection of water, electricity and telephone should not be taken for granted and it is sometimes advisable to use a local agent to ensure that the correct formalities are followed. Production of the Habitation Certificate may be necessary and proof that the property is in your name before the connections can be made, but procedure varies in different areas.

Particularly in the case of a second hand property it is essential to check so far as possible that all debts have been discharged in connection with the property. Pressure can be brought to clear a previous owner's debts and it is advisable to cover such a situation in the contract.

WILLS

A will in Portugal is very advisable once a property has been acquired. Without a will, probate in Portugal is very protracted. Husband and wife each need to make a will personally before a Notary, but it is a relatively simple procedure. It is advisable not to mention a specific property and it is also advisable to exclude your Portuguese property from your English will.

APARTMENTS OR FLATS

The purchase procedure of flats is essentially the same as a house except that they are held freehold and described in detail with areas in the Horizontal Property Deed. This will include the regulations and use of the building as a whole.

There may be a long delay between completion, occupation and final transfer of title and as mentioned earlier a retention in the order of 25 per cent is appropriate until clean title is transferred.

The management of the flats will be carried out by an administrator, who is appointed by the developer for a period of two years and a charge is made for his services. A meeting of the owners or their representatives is held each January to approve the previous year's accounts and budget for the next year. The administrator can be removed except where the original developer remains in control, when it is not possible.

LETTING

Income from your investment is desirable if you wish to cover some or all of your expenses or indeed if you require a return on your money other than the pleasure derived from your own occupation. There are several methods of realising rental and the amount will depend upon location, size, facilities and your own personal requirements:

1. Contracting the property to an agency for a set period on agreed terms, reserving time for your own occupation. A few companies will give a guaranteed sum for the period but this is likely to be low to allow for voids. Most will agree rates and pay as and when they effect lettings. An agreement should be drawn up covering the terms although most firms will have a standard agreement which should be checked carefully, if necessary by a lawyer. Try to select large, well established organisations such as The Travel Club, Upminster, Meon Travel, American Express etc.

2. Do It Yourself. This method will produce the highest return and you can have some selectivity about who uses your property. Advertising in the national press, *The Lady* and golf magazines will produce response and lettings but can be quite expensive over a twelve month period. There are also specialist overseas property magazines published three or four times a year and you can buy space for the year with a photograph. These I have found effective and the main ones are *Private Villas* and the *Villa Abroad. Villa Match* is a computer based system and advertises in the press and on Teletext.

Whatever media you use, lettings will be effected and trial and error will, I am afraid, be the only judge of the best method for your property. While this method will produce the best return it inevitably takes more time and trouble.

Watch your tax position! There is double taxation relief but the Predial tax may not be taken into account and any agent you use is bound to make a return of any lettings he effects on your behalf.

Buying or starting a business

Anyone can set up business as an individual or through a company and trade in Portugal, but certain procedures need to be followed and it will be necessary to register for tax for the income received in Portugal.

The Foreign Investment Institute based in Lisbon is a government body which controls and grants permissions to foreigners to set up business.

For projects of less than 10 million escudos a simple application is all that is required and approval will usually be granted within 60 days. For larger schemes a more detailed application is required providing cash flow projections and other detailed information, for which, if properly submitted, consent will be given.

Proof of residence in the United Kingdom or other common market country is necessary and a Power of Attorney to a Portuguese resident is required to represent you before the Institute.

It is not essential to form a Portuguese company and it is quite possible to trade as an individual. There are advantages in forming a company and they are as follows:

1. More expenses can be written off for tax purposes.
2. There is limited liability.
3. Recognition by customers as a business entity is enhanced.
4. You can obtain a business account at a Portuguese Bank.

There are the following types of companies:

1. Corporation   Sociedade Anonima S.A. – a share company suitable only for large enterprises. Shares are issued, can be transferred and there must be at least five shareholders. The minimum share capital is 5 million escudos (approx. £19,000) and accounts must be published and audited.

2. Company A quota company which is similar to an English limited partnership. Shares are not issued but each partner has an agreed quota or share of the business. This is probably the best format for anyone wanting to start a 'partnership', which does not exist officially in Portuguese law. The minimum equity capital is 400,000 escudos (approx. £1,500) and the shares must have a minimum of 20,000 escudos. There must be at least two shareholders and only the company's assets can meet the company's debts.

3. Limited Liability Single Shareholder Company Formed by a Notary Public and must be registered with the Registrar of Commercial Companies. The Notary must publish the company's statutes in the official government gazette. The capital always shown in escudos must be not less than 400,000 escudos. Only the company's assets will meet, in principle, the debts of the business.

4. Branches These are set up by registering with the Registrar of Companies in the operating area who will note the articles of association, capital invested, and powers of Directors. This enables a company to conduct business through the branch which does not have a separate legal standing. The branch may assume no legal responsibility but is covered by the head office status. If the operating parent company is overseas the statutes must be translated and published in the Portuguese Government Gazette.

TRESPASSES Similar in some respects to an English lease, it is drawn up in a Notarial Deed called *Escritura de Trespasse* which sets out the purchaser's rights under the rental agreement.

Most bars, restaurants and small businesses are held under a rental agreement and when sold as a going concern the agreement passes as an asset of the business. The main principles of the *Trespasse* system are as follows:

1. Rental agreements for bars, restaurants, shops, offices or other commercial uses are perpetually renewable and the landlord cannot terminate the tenancy.
2. The rent can be increased annually by the landlord based on a Government fixed percentage, in accordance with the cost of living increase.
3. The owner of the business held under the agreement can transfer the business to any other party with the benefit of the agreement for the premises without the landlord's consent, providing the transfer of the agreement is ancillary to the business as a whole

*Gypsies - a trespass
perhaps!*

and that the total premises are transferred. The landlord will usually agree to a change of use, providing you can negotiate a new rent!

Rental agreements are often unwritten and evidence of letting is merely a receipt for payment of rent. Formal agreements are often very short and are mainly landlords' covenants imposed on the tenant not to change the use, make alterations without consent and leave the premises in good order on vacation.

Be sure that your lawyer checks out as far as possible that there are no debts left by a former owner, as once you have acquired the premises you are liable for such debts!

LICENCES Bars and restaurants require a licence from the local authority (Camara) and it is a straight forward procedure to transfer from one owner to another. Different types of licence are needed for different operations and a separate licence is required for music.

TAXATION A business needs to be registered with the local tax office (Finânças) for tax and IVA (VAT) purposes. Certainly initially an accountant is essential to deal with tax returns, Work contracts need Social Security charges.

COMPLETION Large deposits are often required when contracts for bars or restaurants are signed and handover frequently takes place before completion of legal formalities. The purchaser must then continue trading in the vendor's name and it is not advisable to make any changes or alterations at this stage until final completion has taken place.

Timeshare

Timeshare takes a number of formats but it can generally be described as the right to occupy a unit of holiday accommodation on a regular basis, usually the same week or weeks but in some cases on a rotational or flexible basis. It is paid for in a lump sum with an additional annual service charge to cover maintenance, upkeep of facilities, management etc.

Timesharing should be considered an investment in holidays for the future and not a financial or property investment. It may well produce a profit if sold but this should be considered a bonus.

Most resorts are very well furnished and equipped and usually have restaurants, bars and swimming pools. Quality resorts will be members of RCI (Resort Condominiums International) or II (Interval International). These are exchange organisations which allow you to swap your week(s) for alternative accommodation elsewhere in the world. The same weeks need not be exchanged provided they fall within the same seasonal time band. A small membership fee and exchange fee is charged.

Portugal is the only European country to pass laws specifically on timeshare, decreed in 1981 (355/81) as amended in 1983 (368/83). Thus the system is quite clear but this has not prevented some unpleasant and much publicised high pressure selling techniques, which fortunately have now been largely curtailed at the instigation of the reputable timeshare operators. This was having an adverse effect on business. Three categories of legal timeshare exist:

1. Those formed within Decree Law 355/81. This gives proper title to the property with a certificate from the Land Registry. Units may be sold, mortgaged or leased. A service charge will be levied and usually the developer will obtain a block permission to import capital from the Bank of Portugal as exchange control is required. Property Purchase tax or 'SISA' is not applicable.

2. The Club System   This operation is authorised by the Foreign Investment Institute. Members acquire the right to occupy for agreed week (s) and these are generally operated under English law.

3. Co-Ownership   Co-ownership is when two or more parties own a property. Equal shares are not necessary and the basis, obligations, administration, maintenance, use and sale of the property are covered by an 'Escritura'. Individual responsibility will be relative to the proportion of the property owned. Rights of sale should be made clear, although the Civil Code allows co-owners to sell freely, subject to a pre-emption right to the other co-owners.

When considering purchase verify the following points or ask the appropriate questions:

Be prepared to say 'no' until you are satisfied and ready

1. Check that you are dealing with a reputable developer.
2. Do not sign a contract unless there is a 'cooling off' period of at least five days.
3. Check that the resort is affiliated to RCI or II, although that does not in itself provide any guarantees.
4. Ensure that the contract is clear, signed by both parties and complies with exchange control regulations.
5. Check that the contract states:
   a) Your rights as an owner
   b) That insurance is included in the maintenance charge and the amount stated.
   c) That you are protected from excessive increases in the maintenance charge by having a vote and joint control with the other owners over the management company.
   d) That any references to Portuguese law are to Decree law 355/81 as amended by 368/83.
6. Use a lawyer if you are unsure or unhappy about the terms.
7. Check that your resort is a member of a national timeshare organisation, which like the British Property Timeshare Association will have laid down standards and ethics within which it can operate.
8. Beware if the property is not completed or furnished.
9. Ensure that at least ten or more units have been sold.

SUMMARY - FOR AND AGAINST   A timeshare purchase in Portugal is protected by specific law, and is usually in perpetuity or a minimum of a 20 year lease. No property tax is payable and holiday accommodation is paid for life. Opportunity to exchange locations is available or you can let your accommodation for income. Maintenance and management is taken off your hands for what should be a reasonable cost.

Capital appreciation may not be very substantial and re-selling your week (s) may not be that easy. You cannot leave personal items in your accommodation and you still have the cost of flights or other transport to your resort.

Land and Construction

The attraction of buying a piece of land, building your own house and incorporating your own design ideas is appealing to many people. Doing so in the Algarve, especially if you are not living there, has its own special problems and pitfalls.

Buying the land is relatively simple as most estate agents have a good selection of land, old farmhouses for conversion or a plot on an urbanization. Try to buy with planning permission or an old dwelling on the land as this speeds the process. Failing this, only sign a contract subject to obtaining permission and tie this down in as much detail as possible. Only deal with authorised agents and check out their credentials locally.

The next important and vital step is to get a reliable and competent architect. Obtaining planning permission by submitting the drawings to the Camara (local authority) can only be done if they are signed by a recognised Portuguese architect. Two months is the statutory period for approval or rejection but this is often exceeded particularly since late 1988 when an embargo on major or high rise development was introduced, thus causing a a rush and subsequent backlog of applications at the Camaras.

It goes without saying that a good lawyer is needed but even more necessary when buying land and building. Apart from sound advice on the title, he should draw up a contract to cover any planning or building permissions needed and indeed, at the appropriate point, a building contract with the selected builder. Unless you are tied to a particular builder, who may be selling the land, or you have decided to accept a well recommended builder, it is good policy to get three quotations.

There are several good companies that offer a package deal. They will find the land, prepare plans, obtain approvals and build the house. This is a good solution especially if you are not able to visit during construction on a regular basis, although this is of course always preferable.

This book does not purport to advise on detailed building construction but the following few points are worth having in the forefront of your mind when considering your design:

1. The Algarve is an earthquake belt and consequently houses are built to withstand a force of seven on the Richter scale. Thus reinforced concrete rafts, generally with frames of similar construction and infill hollow pot bricks is the usual standard.

2. Damp, despite the sunny climate, is a problem in the winter and most houses, new or old, do not have damp courses. I strongly recommend a damp course in your design, and consideration given to cavity wall insulation to reduce condensation, another problem in the winter months.

3. Heating again cannot be ignored and there are a variety of options and permutations now available. Wood burning fires installed in the living room, some with hot water or central heating capability are becoming very popular and indeed are very effective. Solar heating is another option for hot water, central heating or swimming pools. Heat exchange pumps for under floor heating or again swimming pools are expensive to install but cheap to run. Air-conditioning is coming down in price but is still very much a luxury and hardly a necessity. Depending on the house and design a combination of the above is probably the right solution as no one system provides all the answers at economic prices.

4. Endeavour through your lawyer, if necessary, to prepare a clearcut building contract which gives a fixed price, only variable under strict conditions, and a firm completion date with possibly a bonus payment for on time completion, as opposed to a penalty for late delivery.

5. Supervision during construction might seem a simple and obvious piece of advice but it is not the strong point of Portuguese architects. The only sure way is to make your own regular unannounced visits or appoint a surveyor to make regular checks. There are a few English surveyors now in the Algarve and some are listed in the Appendix.

Living in the Algarve

Certain important procedures must be followed in order to take up residence in Portugal on a permanent basis. These steps are currently protracted and conflicting advice on the procedure may be offered from different government sources, both in your country of origin and in Portugal. However, membership of the EEC should gradually reduce the bureaucracy.

RESIDENCE VISA This is essential and application should be made to the Portuguese Consulate General in your country of origin, which is listed under Part I of this book. In the UK this is at Silver City House, 62 Brompton Road, London SW3 Tel: 01 581 8722.

Documentation required with the application includes:

1. Photocopy of passport, medical certificate and photographs.
2. Evidence of your intended occupation or not, i.e. proof of right to practice a profession or of employment or evidence of pension or income.

Additional advice should be obtained from the Consulate. It may well take up to three months or more to obtain but once endorsed in your passport, permission to reside in Portugal has been secured.

Nevertheless, it also essential WITHIN 90 DAYS of arrival in Portugal to fully legalise your residence status by registration at the SERVICOS ESTRANGEIROS (Foreigners Dept.) at the local office of Ministry of Internal Administration, addresses as follows:

PORTIMÃO, Rua Pé da Cruz,8, 2nd Floor Tel: 082 25400.
FARO, Rua José Matos,14, Tel: 089 27822.

Residencia certificates require renewal for the first five years on an annual basis and a Portuguese Bank statement will be requested.

MOVING The procedure for importation of household effects and personal items is not particularly complex assuming the shipper adheres to the regulations. The cost of moving an average house from the UK to Portugal will be between £1,500 and £3,000.

THE BAGGAGE CERTIFICATE (CERTIFICADO DE BAGGAGEM) This is the essential document necessary to import personal and household effects into Portugal, Madeira or the Azores free of customs duty and available under the following conditions:

1. That the interested party is authorised to live in Portugal or

2. That the interested party has purchased a property which is unfurnished or, if the party has had a house built, that the local authority that gave planning permission has issued a Habitation Certificate.

The following documents are required by the Consulate when making the application:

1. A list with duplicate, of furniture and effects in English and Portuguese, showing maker's name and serial numbers of any electrical items.
2. A copy of the applicant's passport.
3. Either the Escritura for the property or the *Carta de Residencia* (Resident's Certificate.)
4. A declaration and affidavit in Portuguese relating to the ownership and age of the goods to be imported.

All these documents must be legalised either by a Commissioner for Oaths or a Notary Public (government appointed lawyer in Portugal) before submitting to the Consulate when a fee is payable.

The Baggage Certificate is valid for 120 days from the date of issue and the goods must arrive in Portugal within one year prior to the arrival of the owner.

The items covered by the Certificate should have been in your possession for at least one year and it does not cover the purchase of new items for the accommodation in Portugal.

CARS AND LICENCES

In the spirit of EEC regulations, there is no current legislation on the importation of cars belonging to foreigners who intend to reside permanently in Portugal.

Cars may be used for 180 days prior to clearance. A nominal administration customs duty is payable from 95$ for a small car up to 1,700$ on cars over 2,000 c.c. including IVA. However at the time of writing there appears to be some difficulty in the interpretation of these laws and I would recommend legal advice on the matter! Apparently only import duty is being waived, the car tax and IVA is not.

For temporary visits a valid EEC or international licence is valid. EEC licences are valid in all EEC countries but there is currently some doubt whether a foreign resident still requires a Portuguese driving licence, which has been the case in the past. The Consulate should be able to clarify but in any event Portugal should come into line with all EEC members in time!

EMPLOYMENT PERMITS

To work on a temporary basis a work visa is required to be endorsed in your passport by the SERVIÇOS ESTRANGEIROS (addresses as before under residence visa).

For a permanent permit the authorities require to be satisfied that the applicant has been legalised and any contract must be registered with the Ministry of Labour by the employer.

Future employment after 1992 should become easier for foreigners as the EEC regulations come more into effect.

TAXATION

As mentioned earlier in this section, major taxation reforms are being introduced which will effect both the incidence and collection, the basic principles having been published in September 1988, but not the full details. The present system, as so far released, is operative from 1st January 1989 but is subject to change as Portugal comes more in line with its EEC partners.

Two new taxes replace most of the old system:

1. *Impostos Sobre o Rendimento das Pessoas Singulares (IRS)* which is the new personal tax.
2. *Impostos Sobre o Rendimento das Pessoas Colectivas (IRC)* the new Corporation tax.

The following categories of income give rise to tax under IRS:

A. From employment.
B. From self-employment.
C. From commercial and industrial activities.
D. From agriculture.
E. From investment.
F. From property.
G. Capital Gains.
H. Pensions.
I. Other including games and lotteries.

After allowable deductions and expenses the categories will be added together to arrive at a total base upon which the tax liability will be calculated.

The rate of tax is progressive from 16 per cent on a taxable income of up to Esc. 450,000 to a maximum of 40 per cent on an income of over Esc. 3,000,000 (approximately £11,500 at Esc.261 to the £) The taxable unit is the family, thus combining incomes, although 'splitting' between husband and wife can now be selected and can have advantages.

Liability to IRS for residents in Portugal is on their world wide income. Non-residents are only liable to IRS on their income derived in Portugal from all categories. Residents should also be aware that world wide income includes all income received from so called offshore investments or bank accounts.

A resident for tax purposes is defined as:

1. An individual who spends 183 days or more in any calendar year in Portugal or,
2. An individual who visits Portugal for a shorter period in any year in which he has residential accommodation on 31st December of that year. (This would appear to make all owners of holiday homes, even timeshare, resident for tax purposes if they visit albeit for a short period!)

Deductions such as mortgage interest, insurance, medical, education and other expenses will be allowed against the total tax liability with set limits. Earned income relief will be allowed at 65 per cent of income from employment up to a maximum of Esc.250,000.

Personal allowances as a deduction tax payable are Esc.20,000 for a single person, Esc.30,000 for a married couple and Esc. 10,000 for each dependant.

Pensions up to Esc.400,000 are exempt from IRS and additional allowances available up to Esc.1,600,000.

The new legislation provides that 50 per cent of Capital Gains, less losses from other sources, are to be aggregated with other income to arrive at the total liability for IRS. Shares held for two years or more are exempt from IRS and if held for a shorter period, subject to a reduced rate of 10 per cent. In the case of property held for over two years, an inflation factor will be applied.

However, an important change in the Capital Gains legislation was introduced in 1989. If a private house is sold and the funds reinvested in another property or in land which is to be built upon and intended for private use, within two years, then it is free of Capital Gains tax.

Capital Gains will not be assessed on any assets including properties which were acquired prior to 1st January 1989.

These reforms will bring more people into the tax net and a key factor is the registration of both resident and non-residents through the *Contribuinte* system with the local authority and the relevant issued number. This system stores information on individuals and will ensure that tax returns are filed by all those liable. A *Contribuinte* number will be issued once a property has been acquired.

CURRENCY REGULATIONS

It is illegal for residents or non-residents to import or export Portuguese currency above certain limits which vary from time to time. Esc.150,000 was the limit in 1989 in any one year to be taken out. Foreign currency may be brought in in any amounts. These regulations change frequently but should become more flexible as the EEC membership matures.

BANK ACCOUNTS The type of account permitted depends on the individual's status as resident or non- resident.

Non-residents may open tourist accounts in escudos and it should be noted that debit balances are not allowed and interest is not paid on these accounts. Funds may be remitted from foreign banks and the account used for the payment of rates, maintenance, household and living expenses whilst in Portugal.

Foreign currency accounts can be opened in Portuguese banks in US$; Canadian$; Dutch Guilder; Belgian Franc; Swiss Franc; French Franc; Sterling; German Marks; Pesetas. The equivalent of 5,000$ is required to open such an account with a minimum time period of 30 days and a maximum of one year. Interest rates are fixed by the banks and it is necessary to prove residence abroad usually by means of a letter from the applicant's bank. Cheque books are not issued and tax is deducted at 15 per cent on the interest at source.

Company bank accounts may be opened with authorisation from the Bank of Portugal for non-resident escudo accounts. The Bank will require Minutes of the Meeting of the Company approving the opening of such an account; the purpose of the account; valid signatories and authorised amounts; and copies of Memorandum and Articles of Association translated and Notarised. The Bank will then, when satisfied, issue a letter setting out the conditions of the operation of the account.

MEDICAL SERVICES The cost of medical services is generally high but there is a reciprocal agreement with all EEC countries. Many foreign residents do take out private medical insurance and this is certainly advisable. Alternatively you can contribute to the equivalent of the Portuguese national insurance scheme known as the *Caixa*.

All major towns have hospitals, health centres, private clinics, and Caixa doctors. One should, however, not expect the same high standards as are available in the UK or other European and North American countries, particularly in the hospitals.

SCHOOLS The options are twofold, the Portuguese national schools or the international schools.

The national schools option is not recommended for foreigners unless the child speaks good Portuguese. A residence visa and certificates from other schools will be required authenticated by the relevant Consulate or Embassy before a Form 435 can be sent by the school to the authority in Lisbon for approval. Nine subjects are studied at preparatory level (10-13 years) and eleven at secondary level (13-16 years).

International schools currently number five with another opening in September 1989. These schools all teach in English, which in a way is contradictory to the principle, but in view of the preponderance of English speaking children, only natural. They are free to recruit staff of any nationality which is clearly a benefit in many ways, not least in language subjects.

The **Escola Internacional do Algarve,** located on the EN125 near Porches is the oldest, founded in 1972, and also the largest with 800 pupils from age five to sixteen years. IGCSE can be taken and the International Baccalaureate for sixteen to eighteen year olds is under consideration. There are some boarding places and full facilities for the twenty nationalities including private coaches.

Next in size is the **Colégio de Vilamoura International School,** opened in 1984 and operated by Lusotur, the Vilamoura master company. Pupils range from four to fourteen years which will increase by one year until 1990 when they will be able to sit IGCSE. Extensive improvements and additional facilities are in hand ultimately to cater for 1,000 students.

The **Prince Henry International College** is at Vale do Lobo and has 170 students with 20 per cent integration with Portuguese children. It takes the pupils up to IGCSE standard and has the added advantage of the use of all the Vale do Lobo sports facilities including tennis and football.

Further west of Lagos and near Espiche the **Barlavento English School** is a small private school for all nationalities for ages four to twelve. This school has small class sizes and prepares children for the larger schools.

In Armação da Pera, the **Lusitania International College Foundation** has been open a short time and is due to move to larger premises in Lagos in September 1989, when it will increase its numbers from ten to about forty pupils. This school specialises in older pupils studying for 'O' and 'A' level examinations and antici-pates liaising and co-ordinating with the Barlavento School.

Also in September 1989 the new **European International College** at Silves is due to open. The current equivalent of 'O' and 'A' level and adult courses will be provided, with small classes a priority over all nationalities and academic standards.

Quinta do Lago

Almansil – 8100 LOULÉ
Algarve – Portugal
Tel.: 96588
Telex: 57121 LAZPLA P

CLUB T * RESTAURANT * BAR * DISCO

It is with great pleasure that I invite you to get to know the "T" CLUB which has been opened on the Buganvilia Plaza in Quinta do Lago.

The "T" CLUB was decorated by the renowned artist and designer, PEDRO LEITÃO, who has created for you a fresh and imaginative atmosphere with lush gardens and waterfalls, all under transparent ceilings.

The "T" CLUB consists of a dining room, bar and dance area, and also boasts an outside garden with bar.

The Chef de Cuisine is PATRICK MIGNOT, distinguished member of the international club "Les Toques Blanches" of France. Patrick prepares his menu each day with fresh produce from the market.

I cordially invite you to join us every day after 7 p.m., with the exception of Sundays.

Yours Sincerely

José Manuel Trigo

Restaurant

The purpose of this section is to set out the projects and schemes of relevance to a potential investor and to indicate their type and quality. It does not attempt to be exhaustive as this would be virtually impossible in such a changing situation. It does try, however, to include projects and schemes of quality which will appeal to the external investor or the potential resident. It includes freehold, divided freehold and timeshare but excludes schemes in the two latter categories where the title, structure or management are for any reason considered doubtful.

Aparthotels (apartments on a self-catering basis but with some central facilities) and similar schemes, are not included in this section as most are strictly to let or only have a small element of timeshare. Those of quality appear under the heading of Accommodation in Part III.

Three geographical sections are used, East, Central and West for convenience. Each sector has advantages and disadvantages depending on your requirements or point of view. The Central Algarve, from Faro to Portimão, has by far the largest concentration of new development and therefore occupies the most space. This area has the most attractions for tourists in terms of facilities. The beaches are long, numerous and accessible. There are several golf courses with more planned and the towns provide a variety of restaurants and nightlife.

The East, from Faro to the Spanish border, is quieter with fewer facilities but is likely to see an increase in building and development in the immediate future. At present there are no golf courses but several are planned. The construction of the bridge over the Guadiana, north of Castro Marim, providing fast access to and from Spain, is likely to have a dramatic effect on this end of the Algarve. It is due for completion in 1991 and will link with the new East-West road to be known as the Via Infante, which in turn will be completed as far as Guia (Albufeira), by 1992. It will ultimately continue on West to Lagos.

The west has developed slowly but steadily, having a more rugged terrain and a cooler sometimes windy climate. Three golf courses with more in the pipeline, a more rural atmosphere without the intense bustle of tourism, has attracted different clientele. The distance from Faro airport has been a disadvantage but the new road proposed and the new bridge, under construction, upstream at Portimão, will reduce travelling time and traffic congestion at the existing Portimão bridge.

The East - Vila Real de Santo Antonio to Faro

This part of the Algarve has had least attention from the developers for several reasons. The coastline immediately east of Faro is marshland or fen with islands or sand bars off the coast, making development difficult and expensive. The good easily accessible beaches do not commence until you pass Tavira around Cabanas, where a number of projects are under way and others planned. The eastern Algarve to date has no golf courses. The main attraction in recent years, other than the weather, drawing tourists to the Algarve, has been golf.

However, a new factor will open up this end of the Algarve. The bridge over the Guadiana river connecting Spain with Portugal is under construction and due to open in 1991. It is located some four kilometres north of Vila Real and clearly will increase the flow of tourists into the eastern Algarve. The Spanish have tended to be day trippers across on the ferry from Ayamonte, but once the bridge opens and access is easier, they will stay longer. Other nationalities who have not previously come by road may now do so via the faster Spanish roads from the south, Seville or via Madrid.

I would anticipate some development to take place north of Vila Real, although much of the land between there and Castro Marim is marshland or fen and indeed is a protected nature reserve. A project is planned north of Castro Marim between the EN125 and the River Guadiana which involves an 18 hole golf course, an hotel, aparthotel, 145 apartments, 74 villas and two further villages. This will help the poor economy of this area.

This must be a sector to look at for the future with its good connection to Spain and only about an hour from Faro airport. Three other golf courses are planned, two near Castro Marim and another at Conceição (Cabanas).

VILA REAL DE SANTO ANTONIO

Apartments are on offer in Vila Real and may well make a good investment in view of the impact of the new bridge, although I do not find it an attractive town. It is very much a border, frontier town and like many, over-commercialised and messy.

MONTE GORDO

The longest established resort east of Faro and fashionable in the 20s and 30s when it had two casinos. Now it only has one and has seen more development in the eastern sector than any other area. It has a fine long sandy beach and apartments and hotels have risen along the streets parallel to the sea. This resort town will prosper and the large number of apartments under construction anticipates a growing demand, although many of these are aparthotels, a popular trend in the Algarve.

If you want modern amenities, nightlife and trips to Spain, Monte Gordo has the answer and is likely to be a sound investment.

Moving west the Urbanisation Retur on Praia Verde is a tourist village to let and not a very pretty site. Praia Verde extends from Monte Gordo to Manta Rota and set back in the pine trees there is a large camping site called Torralta. Then we come to :

ALTURA - ALAGOA

A recently opened Waterslide park called 'Aquiline' on the main EN125 road demonstrates the increased demand in this area served also by the new Eurohotel Altura and a rash of aparthotels, apartments and small villas.

This is a new urbanization with one main contractor and numerous others all building two and three bedroom semi-detached and town houses. Some schemes have swimming pools and tennis but the standard is moderate and consequently the prices competitive. The beach, Praia Verde is long and close by.

MANTA ROTA

A small village spread out, with some new apartment buildings. The beach here takes the same name and a sand bar commences running as far south west as Cabanas, Tavira. Shops and restaurants cluster round the beach front and I would expect things to happen here.

VILA NOVA DE CACELA

Set just north of the EN125 here are some pleasant buildings and a railway station. On the main road an estate agent specialising in the eastern Algarve is located, namely SOTAVENTO Imobilaria Tel: (081) 95165 Telex: 56034. They are Anglo-Portuguese and have an English speaking lawyer and architect on hand. They also have an office on the waterfront at Cabanas; Tel: (081) 20277

CACELA VELHA   This is a delightful village overlooking the sea which hopefully nobody will be allowed to spoil. (See main guide page 00)

CABANAS   This is the increasingly popular location four kilometres east of Tavira where new schemes are under way and others planned. Originally a fishing village, now a growing tourist resort where the sea is some distance from the front, beyond the islands and sand banks. Leaving the main road at Conceição and passing the church of Santo Tiago, you pass under or strangely over the railway line. On the right lies the tourist village of Pedras d'el Rei, not to be confused with a similar complex of the same name on the south west side of Tavira at Santa Luzia. Both offer villas and apartments to rent with a range of leisure facilities.

Before reaching the village itself a new development is situated on the left

Quinta Velha.
Distral Gestao e Projectos Imobilarios Lda
Quinta Velha, CABANAS,
8800 Tavira.
Tel: (081) 20420
Telex: 56644 QVELHA P

Agents: Campbell & Gill Marketing Ltd., Fonthill, Trinity Hill, St Helier, Jersey, Channel Islands.
Tel: 0534 27608
Telex: 4192201
Fax: 0534 27608

Quinta Velha   This project comprises one and two bedroom apartments and two and three bedroom houses set around a pool, gardens, restaurant, pub and gymnasium. The design of the houses is unusual in that the local and typical Tavira domestic architecture has been carefully reproduced. The small pitched roofs have four slopes and the elevations have different coloured window and door surrounds.

This young go-ahead development company has acquired more land nearer the sea for future development.

TAVIRA   Tavira is a beautiful town and has not been spoilt by tourism. With the new policy to control development more sympathetically to the environment, it should remain perhaps the most attractive town in the Algarve.

On the main EN125 outside Tavira there are three large complexes for rental accommodation. They are Quinta da Oliveiras with a Eurohotel hotel and tourist apartments at Nora Velha and Quinta do Morgado; all self catering apartment operations.

Most new development appears to be taking place away from the town centre and inland, close to the EN125 but there are some apartments in town.

Above: Tavira bridge

Apartments on Largo do Santo Amaro
Varzea & Varzea Lda.,
Horta d'el Rei, Lote 4.3 DTO
880 Tavira.
Tel: 22505/23639

Apartments on Largo do Santo Amaro One, two and three bedroom apartments on the outskirts of town in a pleasant location.

Urbanization Estrada da Asseca, Tavira
A large complex of 48 apartments in eight blocks, 54 two and three bedroom town houses and 31 individual villas. Construction has commenced (Feb '89) and it is located just south of the EN125 overlooking the river.

Quinta do Perogil
The first phase of this new project is under way at Perogil, due east of Tavira, on high ground overlooking the EN125, the town and coast. A quality scheme of about 73 houses and 140 apartments with facilities which will include health centre, pool, restaurant, tennis, golf range and putting green.

Urbanization dos Pézinhos
North of the EN125 on the road signposted to Fonte Salgada, it comprises 58 villas and 14 apartments in Phase 1.

All the above projects are being handled by:

Seleccao Imobiliaria
Rua Jaques Pessoa, 15,
8800 Tavira
Tel: (081) 22145
Telex: 56080.
Fax: 081 22145

Benamor Golf Course
Located on land just north of Conceição on the EN125, due north of Cabanas, this is claimed to be the last course designed by the late Henry Cotton. Due to commence during 1989 it will ultimately comprise 70 apartments and villas and an hotel.

The Marlin Country Club
Agents: Vilas & Homes,
Praca da Republicana 16,
8800 Tavira.
Tel: 081 23135/23136
Telex: 58837 VILTAV P

The Marlin Country Club   On the outskirts overlooking the town, again just north of the EN125, two bedroom town house are available with communal pool and tennis court. Squash courts, fitness centre and restaurant are planned. There is also a guaranteed rental income scheme provided by the developers. This is a modest, unpretentious scheme at competitive prices.

Residential Parque Apolo
Apolo Lda., Rua da Porta
Nova 34, Tavira
Tel: 081 23467

Residential Parque Apolo   On the corner of the EN125 and the road to Fonte Salgada new development of two to five bedroom houses on a sloping site with good views.

OLHÃO   Much new building has taken place here particularly close to the main road and is mainly housing for the local population. It is not very attractive but cheap apartments can be obtained here.

The Central Algarve
From FARO to PORTIMÃO

Opposite: Tavira

This sector has seen far more development than any of the other two areas. Its proximity and convenience for the airport, its climate and beaches have all contributed to the huge expansion that has taken place since the mid Sixties but more particularly since 1980.

Considerable criticism has been made of the development in this region and much of it, particularly of the high rise element, has been quite justified. High density both on the ground and above has occurred in the wrong locations and appears to have lacked any co-ordinated planning. On the credit side, however, there are many sympathetic, traditional and attractive projects which have become very successful and popular, even within the much criticised and sometimes notorious timeshare category.

There are five distinct areas within the Central section which have their own characteristics and a knowledge of these in outline will assist in making choices before looking in more detail.

The first lies immediately west of Faro and comprises the large estates of Quinta do Lago, Vale do Lobo and the land between. This is an area of low density, high grade property generally commanding the highest prices in the Algarve.

The second almost adjoins the first and comprises Quarteira and Vilamoura. If the above first area is the top of the market then Quarteira is the bottom! In terms of planning and architecture it deserves all the criticism it gets. Vilamoura, next door, a whole new town, is a mixture of sophistication, good and indifferent schemes, both high and low density, a sporting haven and with its ultimate character still in the formative stage.

The third, separated from Vilamoura by the long Praia da Falésia, begins eight kilometres east of Albufeira at Olhos d'Água and extends west of Albufeira some six kilometres. This area includes Balaia, Oura, Montechoro, and São João in the centre where dense development has occurred and is the home of 'hard sell' timeshare. There are by contrast some excellent hotels, first class apartments and timeshare schemes plus some high quality complexes on the east and western ends.

The fourth area surrounds Armação de Pêra within the confines of Praia Grande and Praia de Marinha. A mixed area of good and poor development but worthy of consideration.

The fifth and final section is centred on Carvoeiro which has seen colossal growth in the last ten years and now spreads four kilometres east and west of the original fishing village. Here apartments, town houses, individual villas as well as timeshare are all available.

QUINTA DO LAGO

Quinta do Lago and Vale do Lobo are a few kilometres apart and in their different ways, represent the best of the tourist development concept on the Algarve. Sometimes referred to as the Beverley Hills of Portugal, Quinta do Lago comprises about 2,000 acres of pine forests around fresh water lakes and only fifteen minutes from Faro airport.

The brainchild of André Jordan, now retired, the emphasis has always been on quality since inception in the late Sixties, but confiscation of the land during the revolution held up progress. The last ten years have seen great strides forward with Roger Abraham taking over the reins at Planal, the operating company. The original exclusive concept has been maintained and created around the splendid golf course, originally three groups of nine holes, but recently increased to thirty six holes. The course is highly rated in golfing circles and has hosted the Portuguese Open Championship on numerous occasions. Another golf course has also opened at the south eastern corner known as São Lourenço which has been acquired by the Trusthouse Forte group who are building a new hotel also to be called the São Lourenço.

Another eighteen hole course is to be constructed due east of the existing courses, giving a total of seventy two holes in all. This will make Quinta do Lago the largest and perhaps the finest golf resort in southern Europe. Individual villa plots are available in and around the courses often with views over the various lakes.

Development projects within the estate include the Bovis Lakeside Village, Bovis São Lourenço Apartments, Vilar do Golf, Four Seasons Country Club and Fairways scheme, Victory Village Club and Quinta do Lago Country Club. The principal facilities include:

Quinta do Lago Country Club   A selection of one, two and three bedroom apartments plus penthouses overlooking the Ria Formosa estuary fitted to a very high standard, where the purchase of weeks in perpetuity entitles the owner to membership of the club. The facilities include a restaurant, bar, snooker room, squash courts, gymnasium, sauna and steam rooms, indoor pool and guaranteed starting times at reduced green fees at Quinta do Lago golf course.

Quinta do Lago Country Club
Quinta do Lago Services Ltd.
P.O.Box 52, Almancil 8106.
Tel: (089) 96562
Telex: 56076 QTLAGO P
Fax: (089) 96574

Country Club Membership Services Ltd.,
106-110 Brompton Road Knightsbridge, London SW3 1JJ.
Tel: 01 581 9555
Telex: 21806 CCMS G
Fax: 01 581 9410

Hotel Quinta do Lago
Almancil, 8100 Loulé.
Tel: (089) 96666
Telex: 57118 (HOQDL P)

Hotel Quinta do Lago   This five star hotel, owned by a Saudi prince, is operated by Orient-Express Hotels. It has 141 rooms, 9 suites, Presidential suite with private pool, air conditioning and satellite TV, heated indoor and outdoor pools, tennis courts, billiards room, health club and function room for up to 200 people.

It is superbly equipped and finished, having delightful grounds with views over the Ria Formosa estuary. There are two high class restaurants.

Shops

The 'Buganvilia Plaza' at the entrance to Quinta provides modern pedestrian shopping with supermarket, bank, restaurant and boutique shops with ample parking facilities.

The 'Q' Line Boutique adjoins the golf practice ground and sells sports equipment and leisure wear.

Apart from golf, horse riding is catered for at the Pinetrees Riding Centre on Avenida do Lago and windsurfing on the main lake at the end of the same Avenida.

Quinta do Lago golf course

HOT PROPERTY IN SPAIN & PORTUGAL

A VILLA OR APARTMENT FROM £50,000 TO £400,000.

In an unspoilt corner of Southern Spain, on the very tip of the Costa Calida, you'll find a Bovis Abroad property in the sun that not only lives up to your dream, but suits your pocket, too. ● Perhaps Portugal would be more to your liking? In Quinta do Lago – one of the most exclusive areas of the Algarve – you also have a wide choice of superbly designed and constructed properties.

LA MANGA CLUB is now rated by many as the most prestigious resort in Southern Spain. And who could guess from its traditional clusters of Andalucian-style villages, spread over 1,200 acres of green and lush land, that here lie some of the most outstanding leisure and sporting facilities in the world? ● For golfers, it's a paradise – with two championship courses. For tennis fans, there's the David Lloyd Racquet Centre. Then, of course, there are beaches, beach club and all manner of watersports. There is a riding centre, a fitness centre and any amount of bars, clubs and restaurants to enjoy when the sun goes down.

LAKESIDE VILLAGE in Quinta do Lago overlooks a calm lake and is surrounded by landscaped gardens, streams and bougainvillea. Nearby is a superb championship 36-hole golf course, home of the Portuguese Open.

SÃO LOURENÇO also in Quinta do Lago, is set upon a wooded hillside, overlooking a beautiful lake. Below, the new 18-hole championship golf course (designed by leading American architect, Joseph Lee) is a short putt away. ● For both Algarve locations, the choice of activities are as varied as at La Manga Club, for adults and children alike. Golf will be the key attraction for many. For those seeking other diversions there's both the lake and the rolling Atlantic to provide watersports of every kind. There's tennis, horse riding, and, of course, a wide range of restaurants, clubs, discos and nightclubs. ● Contact Bovis Abroad now. And start making plans for your home in the sun.

Bovis

**Bovis Abroad Ltd.,
Liscartan House,
127 Sloane Street,
London
SW1X 9BA.
01-823 8000.**

P&O Group

Restaurants, Bars and Clubs

Located adjoining the Hotel Quinta do Lago, Shepherd's has attained a high reputation for cuisine with its fashionable and exclusive Patio Club discotheque next door.

Other restaurants include the Pergola alongside the main lake, the Belvedere at Vilar do Golf and at Club 'T' with dancing within the Buganvilia Plaza shopping centre. The Plaza also houses a discotheque for the younger generation called 'Trigonometria'.

It will be some years before Quinta do Lago as a project is completed as it continues to grow and improve, but there is little doubt that its present high standards will be maintained under the existing management who say "The ultimate objective is to make Quinta do Lago the finest resort in southern Europe".

Bovis Lakeside Village
Bovis Abroad, Quinta do Lago, Almancil, 8100 Loulé.
Tel: 089 94794
Telex: 56311 ATDL P

62 Brompton Road, London, SW3 1BW
Tel: 01 225 0411
Telex: 8812778 LMCC G

Bovis Lakeside Village This attractive development is situated between the windsurf lake and the seventh hole on the C nine of the golf course. Bovis International Ltd, a renowned construction company and part of the P & O Group have created a pleasant village atmosphere. They have built a range of high quality houses from one and two bedroom apartments, two and three bedroom attached villas to three and four bedroom detached villas all for sale freehold.

Bovis São Lourenço

This latest sector of Quinta do Lago is set within the new São Lourenço golf course designed by American golf architect Joseph Lee. Bovis are constructing an hotel for Trusthouse Forte together with one two and three bedroom apartments. These are laid out in a crescent shape overlooking the golf course. They are for sale freehold and owners will have the right to join the new golf club.

Bovis' high standards of quality and finish are evident throughout.

Four Seasons Country Club
Quinta do Lago.
Apt 58 ,8106 Almancil
Tel: 089 94326
Telex: 56715 FSGOLF P

Four Seasons Country Club A concept of town houses and apartments sold on a weekly basis in perpetuity, entitling the owner to the full facilities of the club. These include reserved starting times for golf at reduced green fees, tennis, squash, billiards, gymnasium, sauna, indoor and outdoor heated pools, jacuzzi, restaurant bar and shops. Attractive traditional houses are set in well laid out grounds.

The main clubhouse is tastefully decorated in Moorish style architecture and the club was developed and now run by an Irish property company McInerney Plc. This is timeshare by any other name but up-market with first class management, very popular and successful. Members can elect their own board of management.

*On rare occasions something exceptional is
offered to the real estate market and when this
happens there follows an opportunity that should
rarely be missed.* **Encosta do Lago's** *outstanding
location permits it to enter this category.*

**ENCOSTA
DO LAGO**
Quinta do Lago

Once through the private entrance of
Encosta do Lago*, elegant homes and luxurious
apartments will grace the hillside creating the most
exceptional, freehold development yet seen in
the area of Quinta do Lago.*

*These exclusive properties will be carefully
protected by* **Encosta do Lago's** *own security
guards ensuring only the residents, and those
privileged enough to be invited, will enjoy the
distinctive privacy that is* **Encosta do Lago** *.*

Encosta do Lago, **Empreendimentos Imobiliários, Lda**

Rua da República, 52 1º. A e B. Almancil, 8100 Loulé, Algarve, Portugal.

Tel: 089 97370 / 97376 / 97382. Telex: 58802 ABCLDC. Fax: 089 95705

ATELIER DO SUL - 3209

Four Seasons Fairways
Quinta do Lago.
Apartado 259,
8106 Almancil.
Tel: (089) 94326/94649
Telex: 56715 FSGOLF P

U.K. Four Seasons Resorts,
43 Harwood Road, London
SW6 4QP
Tel: 01 736 0060
Telex: 263406 FSGOLF G
Fax: 01 384 1592

Victory Village Club
Quinta do Lago,Almancil
8100 Loule.
Tel: (089) 94629
Fax: (01) 575358
Telex: 56721 VVCLUB P

Head Office: Imalgarve Lda.
Rua Castilho,75-1 Esq.
1200 Lisboa, Portugal.
Tel: (01)540780
Fax: (01)575358
Telex: 15127 SAFER P

Vilar do Golf
Quinta do Lago, Almancil
8100 Loule.
Tel: 089 96647/685/615
Telex: 58864 VILARG P
SALE TO TRAFALGAR
HOUSE IMMINENT!

Encosta do Lago
Empreendimentos
Imobiliarios Lda.
Rua da Republica, 52 1.
A e B Almancil, 8100 Loule.
Tel: 089 973370/76/78
Telex: 58802
Fax: 089 95705

Four Seasons Fairways   A short distance from the Country Club and bordering the golf course, this is a new development of 130 two and three bedroom villas being sold on a both a freehold and divided freehold basis, called 'Fairshare'. This differs from timeshare in that the owner has title to a percentage, say 25 per cent, of the property and use of in the same proportion.

The clubhouse and facilities include indoor and outdoor pools, jacuzzi, saunas, solarium, squash, tennis, snooker, bar and restaurant.

The same high standards of finish and service expected of McInerney are again in evidence.

Victory Village Club   Located close to the Ria Formosa Nature reserve, the Quinta do Lago Hotel, Shepherds restaurant and Patio Club, the Victory Village club is in a prime position.

It comprises freehold apartments, one and two bedroom, three and four bedroom villas, all laid out in cluster terraces around a central clubhouse and swimming pool facility.

The standard of finish is high and as an investment there is little doubt that it will perform well.

Vilar do Golf   A development recently acquired by Trafalgar House Europe within Quinta do Lago of 180 apartments on rental basis. The square uninspiring buildings are gathered on the golf course and supported by a reception with supermarket and boutique and Restaurant Belvedere. There are three swimming pools, tennis, squash and a sauna with discounted golf and other facilities on Quinta.

Encosta do Lago   This is a small and exclusive development with freehold building plots ranging from 800 square metres to over 2,000, the plots totalling 55 in all.

To complement them, later in 1989, there will be luxury two and three bedroom apartments with a pool, restaurant, tennis courts and superb landscaping which will be started immediately so that it will be available to the first residents. There will be a total of 100 apartments in three phases, two bedrooms of approximately 135 square metres and three bedrooms of approximately 160 square metres.

The villas can cover 30 per cent of the plot area and the main and only entrance will have 24 hour security and optional house alarm/security systems.

VALE DO LOBO.
WOULDN'T YOU JUST
LOVE TO STAY HERE
FOREVER?

(AS LITTLE AS £5000 SAYS YOU CAN!)

For the past 20 years, the rich and the famous have been beating a path to Vale do Lobo, unashamedly the most luxurious development in the Algarve. Just one visit will tell you why. Bordering the Atlantic, this spacious 1000-acre site has been beautifully landscaped to provide a superb environment.

The challenging 27-hole golf course, designed by the late Sir Henry Cotton, is one of the most scenic in Europe.

Here, too, is the famous Roger Taylor Tennis Centre, with its 12 championship courts, swimming pool, delightful terrace bar and restaurant. And now with the Barrington Club, acclaimed as one of the most glamorous and well equipped health and fitness centres, Vale do Lobo offers the finest range of sporting and leisure facilities in Portugal.

Elliott is the direction to go

Drive into Vale do Lobo and you'll be immediately impressed by the sheer space and freshness wherever you look. Moorish-style villas set in an oasis of multi-coloured shrubs and flowers, and acres of lush green fairways. Right on the sea's edge is the hub of Vale do Lobo – the Praça, a small intimate centre of shops, restaurants, pavement cafés, nightclub, pub and cocktail bar, the magnificent Rotunda Pool and here too you will find Elliott's office, open 7 days per week.

It costs very little to stay forever

Through Elliott Co-ownership, a magnificent villa in this sought after location can be yours for as little as £5000 and as a member of the Vale do Lobo Owners' Club, you get substantial discounts on all the facilities, including half price golf and tennis as well as enjoying all the services you would expect from a 5 star resort. Your holiday requirements such as golf bookings and

shopping are co-ordinated through Elliott's London Office, together with flight and car hire arrangements, specially tailored for you at competitive prices.

It's all part of the Elliott service – a personally run on-the-spot management service, which ensures carefree holidays in your immaculately maintained villa at Vale do Lobo for years to come.

Elliott – our name is our reputation

Call at the Elliott Office in the Praça and let us show you our villas (they speak for themselves). Discover more about the benefits of Elliott Co-ownership and why the majority of our sales result from word of mouth recommendation. If you love the Algarve, you'll love the Elliott way of making your stay last forever.

ELLIOTT

Elliott Property & Leisure Group
Praça do Lobo, Vale do Lobo, Algarve
Tel: (089) 94444 ext 5414
Head office and Showroom at
31 St George Street, London W1R 9FA
Tel: 01-491 2677

Vale do Lobo
Vale do Lobo Lda. Almancil
8100, Algarve.
Tel: (089) 94444
Telex: 56844
Fax: 94712 (Administration
& Construction)

Sturgis International
(London representative
office) c/o Sally Viking Line,
81 Piccadilly, London W1Y
9HF.
Tel: 01 495 3686

Vale do Lobo Perhaps the best known of the tourist complexes on the Algarve, Vale do Lobo was the dream and concept of Sir Richard Costain. In the late Sixties in a joint venture with Trusthouse Forte, the golf course designed by Henry Cotton was built together with the Hotel Dona Filipa and the first of the houses. Unfortunately Sir Richard died seeing few of his ideas put into practice. The problems caused by the revolution of 1974 forced Costains Construction to sell. In 1978 Sander van Gelder, a successful Dutch jeweller bought the Vale do Lobo company. He set it on a new path and revised the original plans.

The existing development comprises some 1,000 villas, apartments and town houses all to a high standard many of which front the existing 27 hole championship golf course, where another nine are to be added.

Other sport and leisure facilities include the Roger Taylor Tennis Centre, Clube Barrington Sport and Health Centre, driving range, croquet lawn, cricket pitch, bowling green, football/hockey field and a supermarket.

The Praça, or courtyard is adjacent to the beach and is a focal meeting point. Here there is an English style pub serving medium price meals and snacks together with three other more expensive restaurants, kiosks and boutiques.

Adjoining is the Rotunda complex with two swimming pools and restaurant and in the evening a discotheque in the Kasbah Night Club.

Future plans are ambitious. Apart from further villas four hotels are planned, a marina, shopping mall, conference facilities, new golf clubhouse and reception taking the project well in to the 1990s.

Elliott Co-Ownership
Vale do Lobo.
Elliott Property and Leisure
Group Ltd., Praca do Lobo,
8100, Vale do Lobo.
Tel: 089 94444 Ext 5414
Telex: 264875
Fax: 089 96801

Elliot Co-Ownership The Elliott Property and Leisure group operate co-ownership or divided freehold within the Vale do Lobo complex. Their office situated in the main Praca will provide full details of the properties available currently in three locations on the estate.

Through this scheme you can own a share of the freehold title as explained in the general section on timeshare types and concept.

Elliott's operation gives participants the full use of the wide and varied facilities available through Vale do Lobo club membership, the Roger Taylor Tennis Centre, Clube Barrington Sports and Health Centre including discounts on the above facilities and in Vale do Lobo restaurants.

Travel, rental and resale services are also available with automatic membership of R.C.I., the holiday exchange organisation.

Salinas
Country Club

The Algarve, on Portugal's sunny south coast, is now the most desired destination for family vacations and for permanent retirement.

And among the Algarve's most talked-about holiday developments is the incomparable Salinas Country Club.

This imaginative project occupies a privileged position alongside Quinta do Lago, the country's most exclusive and luxurious resort. Its villas, set among landscaped gardens and seven hectares of unspoiled pine woods, enjoy breathtaking sea views and look out over the famous Quinta do Lago golf course. All the wonderful pleasures of the

Aerial view of site

Algarve-swimming, sailing, windsurfing, golf, tennis and much, much more - are close at hand. And best of all, a quality home of your own at the exciting Salinas Country Club can cost considerably less than you might think.

For further information and colour brochure write to:
Salinas Country Club, Rua Cristóvão P. Norte, Apartado 11, Ribeiro, 8106 Almancil Codex, Algarve, Portugal. Telephone: (089) 97405/97220/94922. Fax: (089) 97779. Telex: 56301 GELDER P.

3552 ATELIER DO SUL

The villas are built and fitted out to a very high standard, some overlooking the golf course, others close to the Roger Taylor Tennis Centre. Full management and maintenance is included and very flexible periods of occupation can be acquired from one to six weeks or more, not necessarily concurrent.

Dunas Douradas   Situated between Quinta do Lago and Vale do Lobo, this project comprises 360 apartments, village houses and individual villas. In a fine location reaching down to the beach, facilities at the centre include a huge Roman style swimming pool, restaurant, bar, mini-market and tennis courts. A sports complex, restaurants and shops will follow in later phases.

This is a quality development undertaken by the Sande Group, owners of the largest construction company in Norway. Mortgage finance is available plus travel, letting and management services.

Dunas Douradas
Sitio do Garrao, Apartado
164, 8106 Almancil Loule.
Tel: 089 96323
Telex: 56400 DUDOU P
Fax: 089 96371

Sande Group UK.,
P.O.Box 170 Amersham,
Buckinghamshire HP7 0RU,
England
Tel: 0494 713920
Telex: 838995 NORPOL G
Fax: 0494 711248

Sandegruppen A.S.
OVRE Hopsnesvei 1,
Postboks 1137,
5001 Bergen, Norway
Tel: 05 135100
Telex: 40400 CESAM N
Fax: 05 134715

Vale do Garrão   This scheme is situated in the valley adjoining Dunas Douradas and being carried out by a local developer. Individual villas, town houses both two and three bedroom plus an aparthotel are situated among the pines. Three pools, restaurant and tennis courts are all available.

This development fills the middle ground gap between the top of the market and lower priced properties.

Vale do Garrão
Apartado 55, Almancil 8106.
Tel: 089 94593/94294
Telex: 56265 Garrao P

Salinas Country Club   Run by Raymond van Gelder who has been developing in the Algarve for eleven years, this is his third project, following Quinta da Salinas and Pinheiros Altos.

Consent has now been obtained on additional land which adjoins Quinta do Lago and the golf course for fourteen villa plots and sixty apartments, which will be a mixture of freehold, timeshare and quarter share. The clubhouse will incorporate a pool, squash courts, snooker, a bowling green, a putting green and a lake.

This is a high quality development in a prime area and clearly a sound investment for future growth.

Salinas Country Club
Sitio do Ancão, Apartment
359 Almancil 8100.
Tel: 089 96245
Telex: 56470 SALI P

Vilas Alvas
Apartado 286, Almancil
8106 Loule.
Tel: 089 96810
Telex: 56302 ALVAS P

Vilas Alvas   On either side of the road that leads to Garrão, Dunas Douradas and the famous Julias beach bar, this low density scheme comprises 90 individual villas and 40 apartments, hotel and a clubhouse. Facilities include restaurant, pub, squash, sauna, swimming pools and tennis courts.

A different style of house design is promoted here and these properties are aimed at the top end of the market.

Club do Ancão
Vilago -Sociedade
Constructora do Ancao Lda.
Tel: 089 96194 22358

Club do Ancão   This project next to Vale do Garrão has a similar concept, comprising villas, apartments and the usual facilities.

HINTERLAND

There are a few projects inland in the hills, and plots and farmhouses are available through agents. As the coastal areas become more developed the foothills are becoming more popular particularly with long stay visitors or residents.

Goldra
Urbanization da Goldra,
Valados, Santa Bárbara de
Nexe, 8800 Faro.
Tel: 089 90542
Telex: 57131

Head Office: Praia da
Carvoeiro 8400 Lagoa.
Tel: 082 57333

Goldra   This is a new development in the Santa Bárbara hills near Loulé with superb panoramic views over a large stretch of the coast and only ten kilometres from Faro airport. There are only twentytwo plots with a social area comprising restaurant, tennis, pools and fitness centre. More suitable as a permanent home but high up and exposed in the winter months.

Santa Catarina
Gonchina, Near Loule

Santa Catarina   A new complex of detached and town houses which seems slow to make progress. Shops, pools and other facilities are promised. Located at Goncinha due south and close to Loule.

Quinta do Gonchina
Gonchina, Near Loulé.
Tel: 089 83527

Quinta do Gonchina   A modest small scheme of villas and town houses opposite Santa Catarina. Convenient to Loule.

QUARTEIRA & VILAMOURA

Apart from the broader Albufeira area, this region within the Loulé district has seen more dense development and at a faster rate than any other area. The choice is therefore vast and for this simple reason I have been very selective in my choice of projects for your attention. Quality has been my criterion.

Almost merging together and separated only by a major road and the football ground, they do have quite different characteristics and cater for different tastes. Let us look at Quarteira first:

Quarteira

This former fishing village has had much adverse criticism in recent years due to its extraordinarily dense and continuing development. It does however remain very popular with the cheaper end of the tourist market despite tower cranes, noisy building work, road works, general mess and dust.

The on-going construction works appear to assume an insatiable demand for apartments to purchase or to rent in aparthotel format.

The dual carriageway which enters from the north east is lined with new apartment blocks on both sides. On the other western side bordering Vilamoura, numerous blocks are being erected. Behind the new relief road and to the rear of the front, huge blocks are up and going up, extending into the hillside.

Candidly I would not advise anyone to purchase an apartment in Quarteira unless you have a very special or particular reason. From an investment and commercial viewpoint it would be foolhardy. A villa on the fringe or an old farmhouse is a different matter and would entirely depend on circumstances. The local licensed agents are Vendavilla, Algarve International, and Urbinvest all to be found in the services section.

The better quality and located blocks are at the eastern end away from the centre both on the relief road and on the promenade. The choice is so vast that in view of my remarks earlier, I am not listing any blocks.

Vilamoura

From a real estate viewpoint Vilamoura is the creation of Arthur Cupertino de Miranda. In 1965 he formed Lusotor, the company responsible for the master plan and evolution of Vilamoura. Comprising 3,800 acres, approximately 1400 are used for agriculture and 2,600 for urban purposes.

It is in effect a new town built on the sea with tourism as its primary objective. It sets out to offer everything wanted by the holidaymaker, tourist, sailor and investor and it is hard to see what has been omitted.

Whatever your view, it is an enormous project which for Lusotur at any rate, and indeed for many others, has been highly successful. Recently (December 1988) a bid for the company has been made by the Kuwait Investment Office, surely a vote of confidence in Vilamoura and the Algarve.

To get to know Vilamoura and to select your preferences it helps to understand the sector numbering system used by Lusatur:

Sector 1   Surrounds the marina housing the main hotels, large apartment blocks, marina shops and restaurants.
Sector 2   Includes the southern half of Golf Course II and the land to the south and west; a mixture of villas, town houses and apartments.
Sector 3   Includes the northern part of Golf Course II and the land north of sector 2: villas, apartments, town houses, and timeshare.
Sector 4   The largest area around Golf Course I north and south with a complete cross section of all types of property.
Sector 5   Sold by Lusotur and planned as a low rise apartment village due north of the new marina extension, south west of the main dual carriageway. Construction to start in 1990.
Sector 6   The new 27 hole golf course where work has commenced and where the residential land within is yet to be released.
Sector 7   Beach area with no housing.
Sector 8   Agriculture and stock breeding area.

A general plan of Vilamoura showing the sectors and layout is available from the offices of Lusotur in the centre opposite the casino. The following is a selection of the better quality and more interesting projects that have either been completed or are under construction working from the north towards the marina:

SECTOR 4

Aldeia do Golf   Tel: 35344 Telex: 58837.

Aldeia do Campo   Near Rock Garden Sports Club.

Bungalows do Golf   Tel: 33250 Telex: 56884

Prado do Golf   8125 Quarteira Tel: 33250

Varandas do Golf   All the above are grouped near the original Vilamoura Golf Course (now known as Golf 1) and clubhouse and are well established, mainly built during the 1970s.

Mouragolf Village   Avenida do Parque, 8125 Vilamoura. Tel: 34545 Telex: 56233 MOGOLF   A quality timeshare resort and a member of Interval International. Full facilities and adjacent to Golf 1.

Monte da Vinha   Tel: 33786   Duplex 1/2 bedroom. No facilities as yet - pool promised.

Oasis Village   Vilamoura 8125, Quarteira. Tel: 34031   A member of RCI. Good standard.

Parque Mourabel   Tel: 32547   110 Apartments timeshare and rental - mid market.

Parque de Amendoeiras   Tel: 34284   Shops, restaurants, 88 apartments - mid market.

Aldeia dos Navegantes   Vilamoura Tel: 33758   9 Town houses for timeshare - mid market. No package tour operators.

SECTOR 2

Golférias   Tel: 34991   Cluster villas with central facilities on Golf Course 2.

Verde Pino   Tel: 33513   Cluster villas for sale on Golf Course 2.

Jardins do Mar   Agents Urbinvest Tel: 34717/34917 Telex: 56811 24 two bedroom apartments to a high standard in a good location.

Impervilla Club   Parque Impervilla, 8125 Vilamoura. RCI Tel: 89 35372   Apartments part timeshare, part sold. Very central with basic facilities 3 star timeshare rating and member of RCI.

SECTOR 3

Montalto   Same ownership as Aldeia dos Navegantes - 66 apartments for timeshare 1,2 and 3 bedroom. Good facilities and standard under construction. No package tour operators.

Tenis Golfmar   Tel: 34479 Telex: 56008   2 large blocks, central pools etc, 32 studio, 35 1 bed, 45 2 bed. Built 6/7 years ago and well managed.

Villas Romanas   Tel: 34769   Unusual design high quality villas on high ground backing on to Golf 2.

Vilamouratenis Centre   Tel: 33899/34169 Telex: 56407   A large project which at present (January 89) comprises 12 tennis courts and a clubhouse. 110 villas are to be built, a total of 40 courts including one to seat 10,000 spectators, 6 squash courts, bowling green, restaurants, 3 pools, health club and a 60 'suite' hotel.

The Old Village   Montpelier International plc Tel: 35399. London : 17 Montpelier Street, SW7 1HG Tel: 01 589 3400. An interesting village atmosphere in neo-classical architecture with shops and restaurants, houses and apartments. For sale (few left) and to rent.

Solar do Golf   8125 Quarteira. Tel: 089 32542   High class apartments on Golf Course II with Club-Bar and pool over looking Golf Course II.

Mar Sol and Mar-bel Sol   Tel: 33637 Telex: 56942   Good quality apartments, half timeshare half for sale.

Edificios Diamante   Tel: 32432   **Edificios Topázio**   2 apartment blocks both built by well regarded local builder. Good quality, good location.

Solnascente   Under construction (Jan'89) 1 & 2 bed apartments for sale.

Four Seasons   Vilamoura, Apartado 661, 8125 Vilamoura. Tel: (089) 34087/34099 Fax: (089) 35141   This is the third McInerney project comprising 96 apartments and clubhouse located on the 9th and 10th fairways of the Vilamoura II golf course. The clubhouse provides all the facilities found at the other resorts. Starting times and reduced green fees at the two Vilamoura golf courses are included and a further 27 holes are due to open in late 1989. Membership of the local tennis centre is also included.

Clubshare and Fractional membership is available. This gives flexibility between one and eight weeks packages where some weeks can be altered each year to suit the owner's requirements and alternated within the seasons.

McInerney's reputation and record in the Algarve speaks for itself. Their schemes are of the highest quality and thoroughly recommended.

SECTOR 1

Delta Marina Vilamoura, 8125 Quarteira 1 and 2 bedroom apartments in the centre close to the marina, shops and all facilities.

Vilamarina Estrada da Praia da Falésia, Apartado 577, Vilamoura, 8125 Quarteira. Tel: 089 33134 Telex: 57122 VIMANA Fax: 089 33578 Exclusive high quality apartments in blocks on a superb island-like location between the old and new marina for sale freehold. Bearing in mind the prices it is surprising that no heating is included. Vilas and Homes are agents Tel: 89 95435/335.

Algardia Marina Parque Tel: 34766 **Edificio Porto Marina** Tel: 32778/32791 Large interlinked blocks with distinctive turret-type towers close to centre and marina with pool and facilities.

Club Mouratlantico Tel: 34104/34142 Telex: 56731 Fax: 089 34277 Part of the overall concept of the above two blocks but a separate timeshare only scheme of 84 apartments sharing the same pool facilities.

ALBUFEIRA AREA

This sector of the coastline from Praia da Falésia to Praia da Gale includes some of the highest density development in the Algarve, particularly in Montechoro, Areias de São João, Oura and Albufeira itself. It comprises mainly apartments, aparthotels, hotels and timeshare but on the eastern and western fringes there are lower density good quality schemes at Olhos D'Água, Balaia, São Raphael and Gale.

Pine Cliffs Golf & Country Club
United Investments (Portugal) E.T.,S.A. Apartado 246 Almancil 8100 Loulé, Portugal. Tel: (89) 95255
Pine Cliffs Algarve Promotions Ltd. Thames Wharf Studios, Rainville Road, London W6 9HA Tel: 01 385 3344

Pine Cliffs Golf & Country Club This project is located on the coast near Olhos D'Água between Vilamoura and Albufeira. It has been awarded the special status of 'conjunto turistico', which enables it to operate exclusively as a private estate with only one entrance and with 24 hour security. It is the only one in existence on the Algarve.

A nine hole golf course, exclusive to owners and hotel guests, and a 215 bedroom Sheraton Hotel will be the central features of this development, which occupies a spectacular site above the beach where erosion of the red soil and cliffs has created impressive and spectacular canyons. Other facilities include a sports centre with squash, swimming, tennis, snooker, health club, sauna and massage, The beach can be reached by path or lift where there is also a bar.

Individual villas, two and three bedroom town houses, and one and two bedroom apartments are carefully placed adjacent to the golf course or amidst the extensively landscaped village.

The Sheraton Hotel will have 216 suites with separate sitting areas opening on to a terrace. Other amenities include top class restaurants, bars, all weather swimming pool, shops and beauty salon. Extensive conference facilities with full secretarial and communications backup will also be available.

This scheme is innovative, exciting and exclusive. The development company is quoted on the Lisbon stock exchange and is soundly financed and advised.

Aldeia das Açoteias Apartado 34, 8200 Albufeira
Tel: 089 50267
Telex: 56812 SOLTUR P

Aldeia das Açoteias Located above Falésia beach with over 400 apartments and villas this holiday village has the accent on sport. Many famous athletes train here in the winter months because of the excellent facilities which include 400 metre all weather running track, full athletic field event pits and areas, cross country course, 2 tennis courts, putting green and gymnasium.

Pinhalfalésia Empreendimentos Turisticos Lda   Large scheme of apartment blocks, aparthotel, villas with pools etc, close to Falesia beach. Under construction (January '89) but appears to be to a good standard.

> **Pinhalfalésia Empreendimentos Turisticos Lda.**
> Pinhal do Concelho,8200 Albufeira.
> Tel: 089 50237/ 50239

Balaia Village   This development which is an associate of Prowting Homes in England is in a good location close to Balaia beach and opposite the former Balaia Hotel, now Club Mediterranee.
The thirty acre site is wooded and the scheme comprises individual villas, cluster villas, apartments, shops restaurant, pool and tennis courts. The properties are available freehold or on a four owner basis. There may be some timeshare in the future.

> **Balaia Village**
> 8200 Albufeira.
> Tel: 089 50265/50754
> Telex: 56714 BALVIL P
> Fax: 089 50265

Quinta da Balaia   This is a good class project of freehold villas, apartments and cluster houses set in pleasant undulating wooded grounds about four kilometres east of Albufeira. Facilities include pool, tennis, squash and restaurant.

> **Quinta da Balaia**
> 8200 Albufeira.
> Tel: 089 52512/52575
> Telex: 56215 ARNOSO P
> Fax: 089 53519

Aldeamento Alfagar   In the same ownership as Quinta da Balaia but a newer project of 218 apartments both for sale and timeshare. It has its own beach, tennis courts, supermarket, pool and restaurant. Under construction (January '89) but many forward sales and the standard looks good.

> **Aldeamento Alfagar**
> Semina 8200 Albufeira.
> Tel: 54960
> Telex: 56359

Aparthotel Lancetur   Close to Santa Eulalia and Balaia beaches this is an aparthotel with an element of timeshare and a member of RCI.

> **Aparthotel Lancetur**
> Apartado 555 Santa Eulalia, 8201 Albufeira.
> Tel: 54835 or 54837

Ourapraia Aparthotel   The same ownership and similar operation to Lancetur.

> **Ourapraia Aparthotel**
> Praia da Oura, 8200 Albufeira. RCI
> Tel: 89 52655/53721

Forte São João   Timeshare apartments on a hill overlooking the sea close to Albufeira. A member of RCI.

> **Forte São João**
> 8200 Albufeira.
> Tel: 089 52378

Solar de São João   Timeshare apartments a mile from the beach with on site restaurant and discotheque. A member of RCI.

> **Solar de São João**
> 8201 Albufeira.
> Tel: 089 53416

Auramar Beach Club
Areias São João,
8200 Albufeira.
Tel: 53337
Member of Interval
International.

Auramar Beach Club   30 year timeshare apartments with flexitime and part of large hotel cliff top complex with many facilities.

Clube do Monaco
Cerro da Lagoa,
8200 Albufeira.
Tel: 54373

Clube do Monaco   Timeshare apartments high on a hill overlooking Albufeira town and beach with pool.

Oura Hotel & Country Club
Areias de São João,
8200 Albufeira.
Tel: 089 53072/55586

Oura Hotel & Country Club   Still part under construction (January '89) but up market timeshare apartments in complex with varied facilities including shops, squash, tennis, sauna etc.

Montechoro Beach Club
Apartado 761, Areias de
São João, 8200 Albufeira.
Tel: 089 54021
Telex: 58839 ORCLUB P

Montechoro Beach Club   Studio, one and two bedroom apartments on a perpetuity timeshare basis to a high standard. Excellent sloping site down to Praia da Oura beach with two pools, games room, gymnasium, sauna and turkish baths. Owners have the use of facilities at the Montechoro Hotel including 8 tennis courts and 4 squash courts. Also members of RCI.

Vila Magna
Montechoro, 8200 Albufeira.
Tel: 089 53611
Telex: 56228

Vila Magna, Montechoro   A huge complex of 200 apartments, supermarket, 70 shops, restaurants, pool, discotheque, cinema and conference facilities.

Vila Magna
Albufeira Jardim,
8200 Albufeira.
Tel: 089 52085
Telex: 56258

Vila Magna, Albufeira Jardim   Similar concept to Montechoro but smaller.

Vila Magna
Santa Eulalia

Vila Magna, Santa Eulalia   A similar project to Montechoro under construction (January '89)

Vale Navio
Apartado 92,
8200 Albufeira.
Tel: 089 54959
Telex: 56266

Vale Navio   An 80 acre development with a mix of freehold villas, apartments, and perpetuity timeshare. Facilities include pools, restaurant, horse riding, tennis and shops. A member of Interval International.

Aparthotel Alfonso III
8200 Albufeira.
Tel: 089

Aparthotel Alfonso III   Timeshare apartments on 25 year lease basis. Facilities include pool, restaurant, discotheque, squash and sauna. A member of Interval International.

Windmill Hill
8200 Albufeira
Tel: 089 52980

Agents:- Vilas & Homes, EN 125,Almancil 8100 Loulé.
Tel: 089 95435/335
Telex: 58319

Windmill Hill   Freehold apartments close to the centre of Albufeira with pool and tennis courts. Good quality by Danish developer.

Club Albufeira
8200 Albufeira.
Tel: 089 55478/53851
Telex: 18521

Club Albufeira   150 cluster villas for sale and apartments. Close to town centre with three pools, tennis, restaurants, discotheque and childrens playground. Developers offer guaranteed rental return

São Rafael Urbanizações Lda,
Sesmarias, 8200 Albufeira.
Tel: 089 53324/53384
Telex: 56366 RAFEAL P
Fax: 55366

São Rafeal Urbanizações Lda   A high quality scheme of over 60 acres adjoining over 500 metres of beaches and coves. It comprises individual villas, village villas and apartments, all for sale freehold, with restaurants, bars and comprehensive sporting facilities. It is undoubtedly a fine location and is being carried out with sympathy and style, yet it is only a short distance from Albufeira's shopping facilities, restaurants and nightlife. A first class scheme.

Praia da Galé
Salgados - Sole Agents:
Realti S.A. Rua do Comercio,4 Almancil, 8100 Loule.
Tel: 089 97064.

Amoreiras, Torre 2-6, andar-Sala 10, 1000 Lisbon.
Tel: 657161
Telex: 65793 SOBIS P
Fax: 01 657166.

Praia da Galé   This is a major project, underway in 1989, of nearly 400 acres and having 1.5 kilometres of beach. It comprises an 18 hole golf course, a 13 court tennis club, clubhouse and pool. There will be three tourist villages located by the sea, the golf course and by the tennis club each of 200 semi-detached villas.

   In addition there will be 50 apartment blocks of 14/16 apartments each and 144 large individual villa plots. Two hotels are also planned plus shops, a bank, and a cinema. It is a comprehensive long term project of quality.

Vila Galé Aparthotel
Apartado 108, Praia da Galé.
Tel: 089 53724/53774/53831
Telex: 57129

Vila Galé Aparthotel   Six kilometres west of Albufeira, a large complex of 220 apartments for timeshare and rental. Facilities include two pools, restaurant, snooker,shops, bowling and tennis. A member of RCI.

A clifftop development
on the edge of the old world
São Rafael

villas and apartments available

2 km west of Albufeira

superb sandy beaches

bars and restaurant

sporting and recreational facilities

40 km from Faro Airport

São Rafael, Urbanizações, Lda.
Sesmarias, 8200 Albufeira, Algarve, Portugal
Telephone: (089) 53324/53384/54066, Telex 56366 RAFAEL P, Fax: 55366

GUIA

Guia is on the EN125 north west of Albufeira and is a simple unspoilt village providing all basic needs. Albufeira is 6 kilometres away.

Quinta dos Alamos
Santomera Lda., Rua General Humberto Delgado,No.11, Guia,8200 Albufeira.
Tel: (082) 56345-56685
Telex: 56917 TOMERO P
Fax: (082) 56346

Quinta dos Alamos   Situated close to the village just off the Guia to Albuferia road this scheme comprises 81 individual villas and groups of town houses with swimming pools, tennis courts, jogging and running area and shops.

The houses are in traditional architecture to a good standard of finish.

ARMAÇÃO DE PÊRA

Originally the fishing village for the inhabitants of Pêra but now a busy, well established and expanding tourist resort with a fine long beach. There is a good selection of hotels, restaurants and night life and a considerable amount of new development, mainly apartments near the centre. High rise, high density seems to have been permitted here, arguably to excess. To the west there are less dense and higher quality developments. A selection of both types are listed below:

Torre Iberius
Developed by Amandio Dias Lda., 8365 Armação de Pêra.
Tel: 082 33685/6
Telex: 56033 SOTOUR

Torre Iberius   A very large high rise apartment complex close to the centre of town with two pools, sauna, restaurants, bars, and a 52 shop centre. Apartments are one two and three bedroom.

Torre do Alto da Torre
Sociedade de Administração, Comercio e Turismo, Lda., Avenida Beira-Mar, 8365 Armação de Pêra.
Tel: 082 32774
Telex: 57405

Torre do Alto da Torre   An enormous development of eight apartment blocks comprising ultimately 600 apartments, complete with 3 pools, 3 tennis courts, bars, restaurants, and shops.

Urbanization Alporchinas
Conjunto turistico de Alporchinhos Porches, 8365 Armação de Pêra.
Tel: 082 32567/32513
Telex: 57409 CARDUMAR

Urbanization Alporchinas   A holiday village of apartments and villas located between the beaches of Senhora da Rocha and Armação complete with pool, tennis and supermarket. Quiet and a reasonable standard of finish.

Aldeaia Mouristica
Developers Largocil Lda, Rua Luis Camões, Lagoa.
Tel: 082 52562

Aldeaia Mouristica   Large development west of Armação of various villa styles. Little information or sales office open but clearly a major project worthy of consideration.

Aldeia das Quintas
Solinvest, Rua 5
October,59. Portimao
Tel: 082 23192

Aldeia das Quintas   A develoment of 102 studio, one and two bedroom flats and some villas. Facilities include supermarket, pool and tennis courts and is close to the well known Vilalara complex. Two storey height restricted scheme to reasonable standard.

Vila Senhora da Rocha
Apartado P.O.Box 2 -8365
Armação de Pêra.
Tel: 082 32349/32376/
32394/32866
Telex: 57406 SENROC P

Vila Senhora da Rocha   A well established, attractive village development which has a total of 255 apartments for sale freehold or timeshare together with freehold individual villas. Facilities include direct beach access, three pools, three tennis courts, restaurant, bar and supermarket. A good scheme.

Quinta das Palmeiras
Senhora da Rocha
Societe Construção Manuel
Bica Lda Armação de Pêra
Tel: 082 33978

Quinta das Palmeiras   No details available. A very large apartment block under construction (February '89)

CARVOEIRO AREA

A very attractive fishing village in origin, still retaining that feel in and around the town beach and centre. However an enormous amount of development has taken place particularly in the last ten years extending three to four kilometres east and west along the coast and now inland on the west side. Although a lot of individual villas have been built the development has been dominated by four firms: Euroactividade A G (Carvoeiro Club etc.): Jorge de Lagos Lda (Golf & Country Club): Trafalgar House (Rocha Brava, originated by the Comben Group) and Colin Phillips Electrosol Lda (Cabeço das Pias). Listed are the better projects:

Euroactividade AG,
Apartado 24, P-8401 Lagoa
Tel: (082)57262/57266/7/8
Fax: 082 57725
Telex: 57655 MOLCAV
P/57695 PORTE P

Euroactividade House, 9
Galena Road, London W6
OLT.
Tel: 01 748 4446
Fax: 01 563 0174
Telex: 916543 CCRENT G

Carvoeiro Club, Monte Carvoeiro, Algarve Clube Atlantico, Palm Gardens & Carvoeiro Club de Golf

These various complexes and others in the pipeline are the concepts of Euroactividade AG, a Lichtenstein based company quoted on the stock exchanges of Zurich, Geneva and Luxembourg.

Carvoeiro Club began in 1970, setting a high standard of freehold individual villas with a tennis club including squash, swimming pool and restaurant. Situated on the opposite east side of the village the **Algarve Club Atlantico** began in 1982 comprising 52 plots, again individual freehold villas with a restaurant and pool facility.

Monte Carvoeiro on the other hand, started in 1985, comprises apartments and town houses set around a main square with restaurants, bars, various shops and central pool. Another square

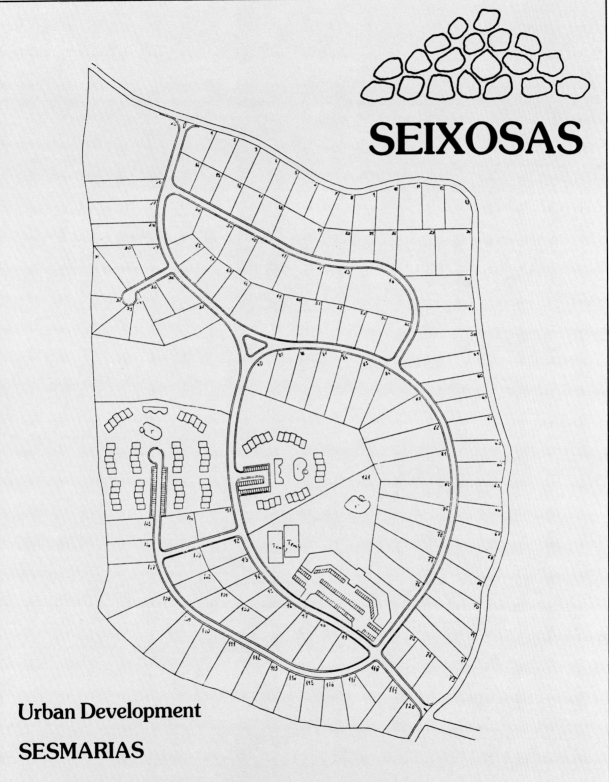

SEIXOSAS

Urban Development

SESMARIAS

A project by Colin Phillips and Electrosol Ltd.
Tel. 082 53687, PO Box 376, 8504 Portimão, Portugal

Jorge de Lagos Village and Country Club

An enviable life style for the discerning buyer

Situated amongst gentle, undulating hills on the eastern edge of Carvoeiro, an attractive fishing village in the centre of the Algarve, we can offer you magnificent luxury villas and apartments plus all the leisure amenities of the Jorge de Lagos Village & Country Club.

You can enjoy an enviable life style at this exclusive development offering tennis courts, bowling green, 9-hole par 3 golf course designed by former Ryder Cup player David Thomas, squash courts, swimming pools, plus clubhouses, restaurants, shops and all just a few minutes from several beautiful, sandy beaches and a riding school.

Choose from two, three and four bedroomed luxury detached villas with own pool, terraced and cluster villas or apartments with shared pools. Prices range from £60,000 to over £150,000.

We have built numerous properties for satisfied clients over the years and offer full management, maintenance and letting services.

Resale properties are also available and we can arrange finance using the Portuguese or UK property as security.

For full literature or further details please phone or write to:

Jorge de Lagos, Lda.
Rua do Barranco, Praia do Carvoeiro,
8400 Lagoa, Algarve, Portugal.
Tel: (082) 57195-57295. Telex: 57463 CSLIFE P.
UK Representative:
The Portuguese Property Bureau Ltd,
Algarve House, The Colonnade, Maidenhead,
Berkshire SL6 1QL. Tel: (0628) 32788.
Telex: 94013273 PROP G.

---✂

Please send me full details of your properties.
Name: _____
Address: _____
_____
_____
_____

Please send this coupon to either of the two addresses above.

provides a supermarket, hairdresser, fitness centre, surgery and other shops. These properties can be bought freehold or on a timeshare basis.

Palm Gardens, situated between the village and Clube Atlantico, continues to supply the timeshare demand but is a small scheme of eight town houses and apartments with central pool,shop, restaurant and tennis court.

Future projects by this company are ambitious. Land has been acquired for the **Carvoeiro Golf and Country Club** with two courses totalling 346 acres. **The Silves Golf and Country Club** of 247 acres is also planned giving a total of about 500 villas and apartments. It is hoped the courses will be ready for play in 1990.

On the **Carvoeiro Tennis Club** land 80 apartments are planned with their own pool. At Monte Carvoeiro another 12 one bedroom apartments are being built.

Another project in Carvoeiro, **Monte Dourado,** comprises 179 town houses, with shops, pools and tennis courts also planned.

Rocha Brava, Carvoeiro

Rocha Brava
Realizacões Turisticas Lda. Apartádo 47, Praia do Carvoeiro, 8400 Lagoa. Tel: (082) 58775/58779 Telex: 57423 BRAVA P
Trafalgar Europe Residential Ltd., 1-4 Portland Square, Bristol, BS2 8RR Tel: 0272 40867/425001 Telex: 44816

Located east of Carvoeiro village, high on the cliffs this project is being built by Trafalgar House Residential (Europe) Ltd, a subsidiary of the public company and one of the largest house builders in the UK

It comprises four villages offering individual villas, town houses, and apartments with divided freehold ownership available in four and six owner schemes.

The many facilities include a tennis centre, pools, shops and restaurants and comprehensive management services which include letting, security and maintenance.

This is a quality development with sound management and to be recommended in an area which has seen considerable growth.

Jorge de Lagos Lda

Jorge de Lagos Lda.
Rua do Barranco, Praia de Carvoeiro, 8400 Lagoa. Tel: (082)57195/57295 Telex: 57463 CSLIFE P Fax: (082) 57624

Jorge de Lagos is one of the best known and respected Portuguese villa builders in the central Algarve and is probably the largest. He has already built over 400 hundred properties.

He is responsible for several of the high quality developments around Carvoeiro, **Colina Branca, Colina Azul, Areias de Moinhos and Vale Covo,** to name a few. He also specialises in building individual villas and pools to order.

He is now concentrating on his 'flagship', **The Jorge de Lagos Village** and **Country Club.** It is situated close to the lovely Centianes beach and will have a nine hole golf course and a village at its centre that will cater for all the family. Shops, restaurants, bowling greens, squash, tennis courts, pools and jacuzzis will form the heart of the resort, with cluster and terrace villas surrounding the village centre. Nearby luxurious homes on individual plots of 1000 square metres are being built complete with pools. Mr de Lagos personally supervises construction and half of the development is sold or under offer. This is a carefully planned and sympathetic scheme.

Cabeço de Pias
Colin Phillips & Elecrosol Lda,
Apartado 376,
8504 Portimão.
Tel: 082 53687.

Cabeço de Pias A project situated inland and to the west of Carvoeiro with fine views toward the Monchique hills and over a new proposed golf course. Comprising 42 detached villas and 18 town houses having access to the common facilities which include pool, children's pool and play area, bar, restaurant, supermarket and tennis court. Individually designed houses are available and care has been taken with landscaping and retention of trees to maintain the rural atmosphere. A pleasant and attractive scheme in a quiet location but close to many other facilities.

Monte Servo Lda.
Rua do Barranco, Praia do Carvoeiro, 8400 Lagoa.
Tel: 082 57225
Telex: 56975 DIETE P

Monte Servo Lda This scheme is situated on high ground above the town and offers five types of houses for construction on individual plots.

Quinta do Paraiso Country Club
Praia do Carvoeiro,
8400 Lagoa.
Tel: 082 57248

Quinta do Paraiso Country Club Mainly a rental resort but some timeshare available. Located west of the town with pleasant apartments and villas with good facilities including pool, restaurant and tennis.

Club Rio
Ferragudo.
Rua Frei Miguel da Anunciação No.31-2, Três Bicos, 8500 Portimão.
Tel: 082 27089/82357

Agents: Villas & Homes, EN 125, Almancil 8100 Loulé
Tel: 089 95435/335
Fax: 351 89 95816
Telex: 58319 VHOMES P

Club Rio A new beachside scheme of only twenty air conditioned apartments set into the hillside. A club format with facilities which will include pool, jacuzzi, direct beach access, restaurant, satellite TV, laundry, telex, and facsimile.

There are fine views across the River Arade to Praia da Rocha. The standards intended here are high and the intention to create an exclusive ambience.

The Western Algarve
Portimão to Cape St Vincent

This section of the Algarve has been developed since the sixties but at a much slower pace than the central area. New development is less intense and concentrated close to Portimão, between Praia da Rocha and Alvôr and further west around Lagos. There are other small pockets but this is generally a quieter, more rural region, although the busy towns of Lagos and Portimão can provide plenty of life and activity.

There are government licensed agents in both of these towns and they are listed in the Appendix.

Edificio Concorde Praia da Rocha.5	**Edificio Concorde** Apartment block with gardens and restaurant at west end of promenade. Backed by Banco National Ultramarino.

Edificio Torre da Rocha Avenida Tomaz Cabriera, Praia da Rocha, 8500 Portimao. Tel: 082 85994/859825	**Edificio Torre da Rocha** One and two bedroom apartments at western end of the front having pool, tennis court, playground, bar, restaurant, shops and supermarket. Under construction (February '89) due for completion June 1989.

Club Praia da Rocha Eurimore Lda., Avenida da Boavista 80-4a Porto Tel: 690481/859555	**Club Praia da Rocha** A huge development set back from the front of 627 apartments with pools, tennis, squash, gymnasium, sauna and shops. (Under construction in February 1989.)

Torre Três Castelos Apartado 27, 8500 Praia da Rocha. Tel: 082 83374 Telex: 57380 PROCON P5	**Torre Três Castelos** Situated between Praia da Rocha and Praia da Vau, close to the beach, this apartment building is available on a timeshare basis and is of good quality. It provides pool, tennis, bar, restaurant and shopping centre. A Member of Interval International and British Property Timeshare Association.

Rotunda do Vau Diamantino da Conceição Silva Lda.,8500 Praia da Rocha. Tel: 25354/26806/ 26779/ 255275	**Rotunda do Vau** 56 apartments plus shops and restaurants under construction in February 1989. **Casa dos Arcos** The same developer as Rotunda do Vau but larger comprising 126 apartments and within 200 metres of the beach. Other facilities include restaurant, two pools and covered parking.

Rotunda Rocha Vau
Rochavaumar S.A. Avenida
Rocha Vau,8500 Portimão.
Tel: 082 26958-83161/2/3
Telex: 57419 MIGFER P5

Rotunda Rocha Vau   A massive development of 258 apartments under construction (February '89) comprising apartments and aparthotel with pools, tennis and squash courts. Restaurant and shopping facilities are also included with health club, sauna, games room and cinema.

This same group plans up to 5,000 more apartments in this vicinity over the next five years!

Urbanization do Vau
Vau da Rocha Construções
Lda.,Rua Frei Miguel da
Annunciação Portimão.
Tel: 22696/260975

Urbanization do Vau   Plots for sale in small scale development in good position.

Clube Vilarosa
Praia da Rocha, 8500
Portimão.
Tel: 082 22211/22327
Telex: 56962 VIROSA P 5

Clube Vilarosa   A very large and comprehensive timeshare resort complex set back from the beach and front. A member of R.C.I. Has a reputation for 'hard sell'.

Clube do Vau
G.P.G Lda.,Rua Dom
Carlos 1.H2. L57, 8500
Portimão.
Tel: 082 27666

Agents: Vilas & Homes,
Edificio Vista
Rio,Lg.Heliodouro Salgado,
8500 Portimão.
Tel: 082 85271/2
Telex: 57172 VHPORT P5

Clube do Vau   Set on high ground, facing south with fine views, this scheme provides individual villas and apartments 200 metres from the beach and a kilometre from the busy Praia da Rocha. The Club has a clubhouse, pool, sports and recreation facilities with shops and restaurants.

Jardim do Vau
Praia do Vau, 8500
Portimão.
Tel: 82 82086/7/8/9
Telex: 57377 CONVAU P
Fax: 082 83915

Emerson Holdings Group of
Companies, Alderley Edge,
Cheshire.SK9 7LF
Tel: 0625 584531/585196
Telex: 669197 EMRSON
Fax: 0625 5857915

Jardim do Vau   A high class timeshare apartment scheme with direct access to the beach. Facilities include pool, children's pool, jacuzzi, restaurant and bar. A member of R.C.I.

Aldeamento Turistico da Prainha
Praia dos Três Irmãos
Apartado 136, 8500
Portimão. (Bovis)
Tel: 082 20561/2
Telex: 57314 PRAINA P
Fax: 082 62029

Bovis Abroad, 62 Brompton
Road, London, SW3 1BW
Tel: 01 225 0411
Telex: 8812778 LMCC G5

Fonte da Pedra
Jointmay Overseas Ltd.,
Wessex Lodge, 11/13
Billetfield, Taunton,
Somerset, TA1 3NN,
England.
Tel: 0823 338100
Fax: 0823 335157

Project Managers: John R.
Evans Lda.,
Rua Judice Biker 35,
8500 Portimão.
Tel: 082 412899
Fax: 082 24765

Agents: John R Evans
RealSol Lda.,
Rua Judice Biker 35,
8500 Portimão.
Tel: 082 26206
Fax: 082 24765
Telex: 57309

The Alto Club, Alvôr
Quinta do Alto do Poço,
Alvor, 8500 Portimão.
Tel: 082 20644/20665/
20679/20119
Telex: 56398 APOCO P
Fax: 082 20558 telfax.

Almond Leisure Ltd., 15
Dover Street, Canterbury
Kent CT1 3DH
Tel: 01 839 4121

Aldeamento Turistico da Prainha   A village with an atmosphere of old and new, Prainha is a well established resort now in the process of rejuvenation and extension. Bovis Abroad are project managing and marketing apartments and villas which are finished to a high standard and available on a freehold basis.

The spectacular cliff top position with its unusual shaped pool, and large grassed terraces offers a bar and restaurant with a lift cut into the rock which takes you to the beach and coves below. Additionally there is a children's playground, supermarket and floodlit tennis courts.

Fonte da Pedra   This small estate is situated midway between Portimão and Lagos, just inland from the village of Mexilhoeiro Grande where there is a variety of shops, restaurants and bars. As a rural development, it offers 31 sites between 2,500 sq metres and 3,000 sq metres for luxury villas with pools. Another 15 sites will later complete the complex.

Many of the villas will enjoy uninterrupted views to the coast and sea beyond, whereas the remainder at the northern end will overlook the hills and Monchique mountain range. The environment created will provide a relaxed atmosphere to be enjoyed for both holidays and permanent homes.

The Alto Club   Close to the attractive old fishing village of Alvôr, the Alto Club, conceived to highest standards, offers individual villas, village houses and apartments on both a freehold and timeshare basis. A concept known as Almond Time offers two fixed weeks and four flexible weeks. The club is affiliated to R.C.I.

All facilities with the beach a few minutes away, include a pool, tennis and squash courts, restaurants, clubhouse, health and sports centre. The Alto Golf Club situated only a kilometre away, designed by the late Henry Cotton, is due to open in 1990 and is for the exclusive use of Alto Club members.

This is a project aimed at the top of the market and looks set to be very successful.

Introducing the Alto Club..

The creators of the now world-famous Penina Estates are pleased to announce the opening of their new project.

"We liked the Algarve and we knew we wanted to come back again and again, but we needed to guarantee the standard of our accommodation".

Alto owner.

The Alto Club, carefully planned for a full two years before construction commenced, is one of the first projects to pass through the Government's strict new planning regulations. This means low density building, height restrictions and advanced infrastructure.

"We feel strongly about the environment. It is vital that a new development blends in with its historic surroundings".

Alto owner.

Charm is a key word at the Alto Club. Located on a picturesque 18 acre site overlooking the sea and situated between historic Lagos and the colourful port of Portimão, the Alto Club has the quaint village of Alvor on its doorstep with people who are proudly independent and have a charm of their own, which is reflected in its fishing tradition.

Ramiro Laranjo, one of the country's leading architects is renown for his work on the exclusive Vilalara development as well as villas and apartments on the Penina and Quinta do Lago estates. At Alto Club, he has preserved the unique character and special charm of the Algarve and yet managed to incorporate everything (and more) necessary for modern day luxury living.

"We thought that we deserved something a little exclusive.

Alto owner.

The Alto Club is securely surrounded by an unusual "scrolled" wall, through which owners will pass freely by a friendly gateman with their own special membership cards.

Onsite, owners will have exclusive use of all the facilities which include indoor sports centre with heated pool, squash courts, gym, solarium, jacuzzi and sauna. A creche for the very young, tennis, swimming pools and exotic gardens for the older, are also available.

Offsite, the beach is only a short walk away. Here you can enjoy a full range of water sports or just be lazy at our own Beach Club.

Additionally, Alto Golf is just 1km away. Construction of the 18 hole championship course, designed by the late Sir Henry Cotton, is well underway and promises to be a jewel in the Algarve's golfing crown. Membership will be exclusive to Alto owners.

The Alto Club has been designed to suit a wide range of choices and budgets. Your own villa in its grounds would cost you approximately £150,000. A luxury apartment can be acquired for one week a year forever, for as little as £3,450.

ALTO·club

ALMOND LEISURE LTD.
Riverside House, 1A The Embankment, Putney, London SW15 1LB. Tel: 01.780 2474

..Exclusive charm and quality

The river, Alvôr

Club Alvorférias
Estrada de Alvôr, 8500
Portimão.
Tel: 082 20240/20247
Telex: 57683 ALVOR P

Agents: Vilas &
Homes,EN125 Almancil,
8100 Loulé
Tel: 089 95816
Telex: 58319 VHOMES P

Club Alvorférias   An apartment complex of studio, one or two bedrooms close to Alvôr beach. It has two pools, tennis courts, bar, sauna, coffee shops and discotheque.

Vila Marachique
Estrada Alvôr 8500,
Portimão.
Tel: 082 20762/3/4
Telex: 57187 CECIRA5

Vila Marachique   A private club near the Alvor where freehold apartments are available. Facilities include pools, sports area, floodlit tennis, restaurant, grill, health club, business and conference centre and children's playground. Although still under construction (February '89) the standards set look high.

Aldeamento da Bemposta
Estrada Alvôr, 8500
Portimão.
Tel: 22173/4
Telex: 573665

Aldeamento da Bemposta   An established holiday village of 78 units of various types with a new phase of 30 apartments due to commence in April 1989. Located inland but near Alvôr village and beach it has a large pool, children's pool and play area, restaurant, tennis courts, minimarket, laundry, TV lounge and entertainment.

BUILDERS, DEVELOPERS AND ESTATE AGENTS

Established for over 10 years in Lagos and with our own offices in England, we offer a complete construction, design and real estate service in the western Algarve.

As major developers we offer villas and apartments on our own exclusive estates. Contact us for more information and a copy of our latest brochure.

GRIFFITHS & GRIFFITHS

Property Developers / Estate Agents

Sales Office – Rua Marques de Pombal, 30, 8600 Lagos, Tel: (082) 60416, Fax: (082) 68898, Telex: 57448 ALVEST P. (opposite Tourist Office)
Praia da Luz Office – Centro Comercial Luztur, Loja 5, Praia da Luz, 8600 Lagos, Tel:(082) 69176
U.K. Agents: – Prudential International, 2 Allington Close, Wimbledon Village, London, SW19 5AP. Tel: 01-947 7333 Fax: 01-947 4390.

Portiferias,
Estrada Alvôr, 8500
Portimão.
Construções Lda. Rua
Antonio Barbudo,16 - 8500
Portimão.
Tel: 082 827215

Aldeia do Biscainhas
Alcalar, Portimão.
Tel: 082 82701 (Frank
Knight FRICS)

**The Griffiths & Griffiths
Group**
Rua Lima Leitão, 19-1 ESQ,
8600 Lagos.
Tel: 082 63224
Telex: 57448 ALVEST P

Sales: Rua Marques de
Pombal, 30-A,8600 Lagos.
Tel: 082 60416
Telex: 57448 ALVEST P

UK: 130 High Street Eton,
Berks.
Tel: 0753 866012/866982
Telex: 848730 ALGRIF G
Fax: 0753 860903

UK Marketing agents:
Prudential Property
Services, International
Division, 2 Allington Close,
Wimbledon Village, London,
SW19 5AP
Tel: 01 947 7333
Telex: 918808
Fax: 01 947 4390

Portiferias   A new apartment complex of 41 units about a kilometre from the beach with pools restaurants and shopping facilities.

Aldeia do Biscainhas   A small attractive development of just 30 plots where individual villas can be built to your own specification. It is located four kilometres north of the EN125 on the Alcalar road at Penina in a quiet rural location. Portimão, Alvôr and Lagos are only a short drive.

The Griffiths & Griffiths Group   Based in the western Algarve at Lagos and with an office in Eton, Berkshire, as support, this company has been operating as agents and developers for well over ten years. In addition to traditional estate agency and representing Prudential International Properties from Portimão west, developments in hand include the following:

Parque do Moinho   Located on the western outskirts of Lagos, within walking distance of the centre and fine beaches, this scheme offers a variety of apartments in three storey blocks comprising one and two bedrooms. Other facilities will include pool, restaurant, supermarket, and hairdresser.

Meia Praia   This development comprises four apartment blocks located east of Lagos and only a short distance from the fine Meia Praia beach and with easy access to Palmares and Penina Golf courses.
    The three storey blocks provide two bedroom, two bathroom apartments, lounge/dining room and fitted kitchen. The grounds will be landscaped and have a large swimming pool.

Colinas Verdes   Four miles inland from Lagos this project comprises 500 acres of undulating hillside with fine views. This is an exclusive development offering high quality homes suitable for holiday homes or more permanent residence. Large plots are available, mostly about half an acre, with a wide choice of villa designs or built to the purchaser's own specification.

Porto de Mós   This is a new project on a 95 acre coastal site offering excellent sea views with easy access to the beach and Lagos.

Waterside Village Gardens
Praia da Luz, Lagos

1, 2 and 3 bedroom apartments and cottages in this renowned village-within-a-village from £36,000 to £68,000.

Ocean Club pool, Praia da Luz

Praia da Luz

Pinhal da Meia Praia Lagos
The first and best located village on Meia Praia beach. 1, 2 and 3 bedroom apartments and cottages from £36,000 to £73,000.

ALPART, Travessa do Forno 4, 8600 Lagos, Algarve, Portugal
Tel: (082) 63721, **Fax**: (082) 60182, **Telex**: 57675 ALPART P.

Lagos harbour

This prestigious development will provide a wide range of luxury detached villas with pools, cluster villas of two and three bedrooms and a range of apartments. The development will include sports and commercial areas and a full management service.

Funchal   Another new development of a small number of detached luxury villas with large pools, all to be built to a high standard and specification. The large plots produce a high degree of seclusion in keeping with the exclusive nature of the area.

The Ocean Club   This village on the beach is immediately associated with two Algarve stalwarts who have been here over twenty years. The very English, David Symington and John Garveigh, opened an office in Portimão in the mid Sixties and have been responsible for most of the development in Luz. They originally developed the Luz Bay Club, no longer in their ownership, but still dominate the market with tasteful schemes like the Ocean Club, where the Waterside Village is the current and final phase.

The Club provides three pools, five tennis courts, restaurant, bars and gardens. The garden and beach sections offer apartments and cottages for sale with a full rental and management back-up service through Ocean Club.

About five kilometres from Luz towards Lagos just north of the EN125, the Funchal Country Club has been developed providing

The Ocean Club, Praia da Luz
Rua Direita, Praia Da Luz, 8600 Lagos.
Tel: 082 69472/69763
Telex: 57474 OCEAN P

Alpart & Ecogal, Travessa do Forno 4, 8600 Lagos.
Tel: (082) 63721
Telex: 57675 ALPART P

Hamptons International Dept. 6 Arlington Street, St James' London SW1.
Tel: 01 493 8222
Telex: 25341
Fax: 01 491 3541

twenty-three individual villas in a prime location with views over Lagos Bay. Although more suited to long term home owners membership of the Ocean Club with all the facilities at Praia da Luz is included.

Another Alpart/Ecogal project (the companies owned by Garveigh and Symington), is at Pinhal da Meia Praia. Their successful formula is to be repeated and again one expects their same high standards.

Luz Bay Club and Luz Park   A large villa and apartment complex set in the village of Praia da Luz comprising some 200 properties. Originally started in 1967 new and upgraded houses are available with the facilities which include swimming pools, tennis courts, squash, sauna, jacuzzi, shops and restaurants.

In parts looking a little tired but improvements are in hand and good value can be obtained from an upgraded property.

Quinta Bela Vista   Set in the highest part of Praia da Luz this scheme comprises smaller two bedroomed houses which take advantage of the views by putting the living accommodation on the upper level. Facilities will include two pools, restaurant, tennis courts and mini-market.

Parque da Floresta   This recent development is located inland from the fishing village of Salema about fifteen minutes drive west of Lagos. Set in over 300 acres, the golf course occupies the lower lying area and provides many fine views and challenging holes. The residential element, on higher ground, overlooks the course. Other facilities will include a hotel and a sports complex with swimming pool, squash courts, gymnasium and fitness centre, sauna, jacuzzi, crèche, shops, bars and restaurants.

The first phase of village houses has been built behind the golf clubhouse comprising two and three bedroom properties. Individual villas in Phase 1 are located around the lake between the twelfth and eighteenth holes.

All owners will enjoy 50 per cent discounted green fee privileges in perpetuity and preferred starting times.

This is a concept for those who want to be away from it all in the quieter more rural western Algarve. The golf course may need a little while to mature but it will undoubtedly attract the enthusiasts.

The development has being taken over recently by Euroactividade A.G., owners of the various projects in Carvoeiro but we understand that Beach Villas are to remain as agents.

Luz Bay Club and Luz Park
Praia da Luz, 8600 Lagos.
Tel: 082 69640-69645
Telex: 57661 LUZBAY P

Quinta Bela Vista
Praia da Luz.
Rustimar Lda., Apt 155,
Praia da Luz, 8600 Lagos
Tel: 082 69891
Telex: 58910

Parque da Floresta
Budens.

Golf Clubhouse
Tel: (082)65333/4/5
Telex: 57173 GOLSAN P

Administration
Tel: (082) 65407
Telex: 58862 QDCGSA P

Beach Villa Sales Ltd
55 Sidney Street,
Cambridge CB2 3JW,
England.
Tel: 0223 353222
Telex: 817428 BCHVLA G
Fax: 0223 313557

2 St Annes Square,
Manchester M2 7HJ,
England.
Tel: 061 834 0700
Telex: 665942 BVMAN G
Fax: 061 834 6145

Salema Beach Club
Salema.
Beach Villas, 8 Market
Passage, Cambridge,
England.
Tel: 0223 311113 or Nos.
above.

Salema Beach Club   Owned and run by Beach Villas of Cambridge, this is set back on the slopes of the village but close to the beach and shops. A small number of apartments are available here on a timeshare basis.

Quinta da Fortaleza
Agents: Vilas & Homes,
Edificio Vista Rio, Largo
Heliodouro Salgado, 8500
Portimão.
Tel: 082 85271/2
Telex: 57172 VHPORT P

Quinta da Fortaleza   Located on the coast between Burgau and Salema this is a new development comprising an 18 hole golf course with villas overlooking the first nine holes. A mixture of town houses and individual villas are being built and the other facilities will include restaurant, driving range, tennis, a clubhouse with indoor and outdoor pools, sauna, night club and discotheque.

SAGRES

Sagres

Little development has occurred here although there is a good supply of hotel accommodation as listed under 'Accommodation' (page 99).

Where dreams come true

A selection of luxury villas
and houses on a choice of unspoilt sites
in the heart of the countryside or set beside
your own superb sandy beach.

Whatever your dream, we have the perfect spot for you!

Quinta do Martinhal

Forte da Pedra

FOR FULL DETAILS CONTACT

JOINTMAY OVERSEAS LTD. Wessex Lodge, 11/13 Billetfield, Taunton, Somerset TA1 3NN, England.
Tel: (0823) 338100 Fax: (0823) 335157
JOHN R. EVANS REALSOL LDA. Rua Judice Biker 35, 8500 Portimao, Algarve, Portugal.
Tel: (082) 26206 Fax: (082) 24765 Telex: 57309

Henry the Navigator Apartments
Vilanorte Construções Lda.,
Campo Pequeno 1000
Lisboa
Tel: 01 779350
Telex: 62743 VNOPTPLP P

Henry the Navigator Apartments   A project located on the roundabout on the main road outside Sagres of two, three and four bedroom apartments with swimming pool, tennis court and children's playground.

Quinta do Martinhal
Sagrimar Empreendimentos
Turisticos Lda
Apartado 14, Sagres, 8650
Vila do Bispo.
Telex: 58701

Project Manager: Frutiger
AG International,
Burgstrasse 20 CH-3601
Thun Switzerland.
Tel: 033 216626
Telex: 921277
Fax: 033 225804

Agents: John R Evans
Realsol Lda.,
Rua Judice Biker,35 8500
Portimão.
Tel: 082 26206
Telex: 57309
Fax: 082 24765.

Quinta do Martinhal   This important project occupies an entire bay in a south facing sheltered location east of Sagres. It has its own 500 metre length of beach and the existing motel and restaurant 'Os Gambozinos' will be extended and upgraded.

The scheme comprises 92 detached villas, 54 terraced houses, a clubhouse and restaurant. There will be a large selection of both villa and terraced house designs to choose from as well as some extra large plots for special designs.

The club facilities will include a coffee shop, restaurant, bar, lounge, large pool and bar, playground, two squash courts, four tennis courts. Additionally there will be a supermarket and newsagent plus reception with secretarial services.

The co-developers of this scheme set out to achieve the highest standards and the project managers Frutiger AG International have the highest pedigree and are well qualified to undertake such a project.

Vale da Telha
Apartado 101, 8670 Aljezur.
Tel: 082 98179
Telex: 57466 P

Somundi Sociedade
Turistica do Algarve Lda.,
Avenida Miguel Bombarda,
163, 1000 Lisbon.
Tel: 01 522638
Telex: 13746 P

Vale da Telha   An enormous development of close on 2000 acres of mainly individual villas. A full road network is in place and all services are installed. A three star hotel, restaurant, bars, shops, riding and tennis and central swimming pool are some of the facilities offered. Accessible preferably from Lisbon.

The Dona Filipa, a splendid complement to all that the Algave can offer, is only 18 kilometres from Faro Airport, and its 147 air-conditioned rooms provide all the luxury to be expected from a five star-hotel. Guests can enjoy the best of all local and international cuisine.

There is a superb 27 hole championship golf course

HOTEL
Dona Filipa
★★★★★
Algarve, Portugal

designed by Henry Cotton, a heated swimming-pool, three full-size tennis courts and 14 kilometres of white beaches. The hotel stands in seclusion amid pinewoods and fig orchards. And now the Dona Filipa guests can play free of charge at the new San Lorenzo Golf course in Quinta do Lago.

HOTEL DONA FILIPA
Vale do Lobo, Almancil, 8100 Loulé, Algarve, Portugal
Tel: (89) 941 41. Telex: 56848 Filipa P. Fax: (89) 94288

Trusthouse Forte Hotels

PART III

ACCOMMODATION AND RESTAURANTS

This section is a selection of the better quality accommodation and restaurants either visited by myself or known to have a good reputation. The restaurants will usually have been in the same ownership for at least three years. It does not purport to be a 'Hotel' or 'Good Food Guide' as there are books attempting to cover the subject, which is of course, ever changing.

Hotels

The Portuguese National Tourist Offices and the local Algarve tourist offices provide comprehensive lists of all hotels, aparthotels, pousadas, estalagens and pensaos, categorised with an official star rating from 1-5. Pousadas are state run, similar to the Spanish paradors, are often in historic converted buildings, very good value and high standard. Unfortunately there are only two in the Algarve at Sagres and São Brás. Estalagens (singular estalagem) and albergarias are of a similar standard to pousadas, but privately run. Pensões are not quite of the same standard as hotels. The following are well established and have good reputations with a four or five star rating: (An asterisk * indicates fine cuisine)

ALBUFEIRA **Hotel Alfamar**, Praia da Falesia, 8200 Albufeira.
Tel: 089 66224 Telex: 56840
Hotel Montechoro, Montechoro, 8200 Albufeira.
Tel: 089 52651 Telex: 56288
Hotel Boa Vista, Rua Samora Barros, 8200 Albufeira.
Tel: 089 52175 Telex: 56204
Hotel California, Rua Candido dos Reis, 8200 Albufeira.
Tel: 089 52833 Telex: 56654
***Estalagem Vila Joya**, Praia da Gale, 8200 Albufeira.
Tel: 089 54795 Telex: 56222

FARO and Area

Hotel Eva, Avenida da Republica, 8000 Faro.
Tel: 089 24054 Telex: 56224.
***Hotel La Reserve**, Santa Bárbara de Nexe, 8000 Faro.
Tel: 089 91234/91474 Telex: 56790
Hotel Riamar, Praia de Faro, 8000 Faro.
Tel: 089 23542/23189 Telex: 58347
Pousada de São Brás, 8150 São Brás de Alportel.
Tel: 089 42305/6 Telex: 56786

LAGOA (Praia da Carvoeiro)

Hotel Dom Sancho, Largo da Praia, 8400 Lagoa.
Tel: 082 57350 Telex: 57351
Hotel Solferias, sitio Mato Serrão, 8400 Lagoa.
Tel: 082 57401 Telex: 57481

LAGOS

Hotel Golfinho, Praia Dona Ana, 8600 Lagos.
Tel: 082 63001/2 Telex: 57489
Hotel de Lagos, Rua Nova da Aldeia, 8600 Lagos.
Tel: 082 62011 Telex: 57477

MONCHIQUE

Albergaria Lageado, 8550 Caldas de Monchique.
Tel: 082 92206
Estalagem Abrigo da Montanha, Estrada da Foia, 8550 Monchique.
Tel: 082 912131
Mon Cicus, Estrada da Foia, 8550 Monchique.
Tel: 082 92650

PORTIMÃO (Praia da Rocha - Alvôr)

***Hotel Algarve**, Avenida Tomas Cabreira, 8500 Praia da Rocha.
Tel: 082 24000/9 Telex: 57347
***Hotel Alvôr Praia**, Praia dos Três Irmãos, 8500 Alvôr.
Tel: 082 24021/9 Telex: 57399.
***Hotel Golfe da Penina**, Montes de Alvôr, 8500 Portimão.
Tel: 082 22051/8 Telex: 53707
Hotel Delfim, Praia dos Três Irmãos, 8500 Alvôr.
Tel: 082 27170 Telex: 57399
Hotel Dom João II, Praia da Alvôr, 8500 Alvôr.
Tel: 082 20135 Telex: 57321

Hotel Jupiter, Avenida Marginal, 8500 Praia da Rocha.
Tel: 082 22041 Telex: 57346
Hotel Bela Vista, Avenida Marginal, 8500 Praia da Rocha.
Tel: 082 24055/6 Telex: 57395
Hotel Viking, Senhora da Rocha, 8300 Armação da Pera.
Tel: 082 32336 Telex: 57492
Hotel do Levante, Vale do Olival, 8300 Armação da Pêra.
Tel: 082 32322 Telex: 57478
Hotel Garbe, Avenida Marginal, 8300 Armação da Pêra.
Tel: 082 32194 Telex: 57485
***Vilalara**, Praia do Redondo, 8300 Armação da Pêra.
Tel: 082 32333 Telex: 57460

VILA REAL DE SANTO ANTONIO (Monte Gordo)

Hotel Alcazar, Rua de Ceuta, 8900 Monte Gordo.
Tel: 081 42184 Telex: 56028
Hotel Vasco da Gama, (3 star) Avenida Infante de Sagres, 8900 Monte Gordo. Tel: 081 44321 Telex: 56020
Hotel Casablanca Inn, Rua 7, 8900 Monte Gordo.
Tel: 081 42444 Telex: 56939
Albergaria Monte Gordo, Avenida Infante D. Henrique, 8900 Monte Gordo.
Tel: 42124.

SAGRES

Estalagem Infante do Mar, Praia da Salema, 8650 Sagres.
Tel: 082 65137 Telex: 57451.
Pousada do Infante, 8650 Sagres.
Tel: 081 64222 Telex: 57491
Albergaria Navigator, 8650 Sagres.
Tel: 081 64554 Telex: 57688.

VILAMOURA, ALMANCIL, QUARTEIRA area

Hotel Dona Filipa, Vale do Lobo, 8100 Almancil.
Tel: 089 94141/2/3 Telex: 56848.
Hotel Atlantis, 8100 Vilamoura.
Tel: 089 32868/32797 Telex: 56838.
Hotel Dom Pedro, 8100 Vilamoura.
Tel: 089 35460/35450 Telex: 56870
Hotel Quarteirasol, 8100 Quarteira.
Tel: 089 34421 Telex: 56809
Hotel Vilamoura Marinhotel, 8100 Vilamoura.
Tel: 089 33414 Telex: 58827/58979.

Vilamoura Marinhotel

Restaurants

This brief résumé of restaurants is selected on the criteria of quality, value for money and reliability. The majority are well established or have attained a good reputation. I apologise to any restaurateur who may be offended by omission!

SAGRES **A Tasca**, overlooking the inner harbour.   Tel: 082 64177
Sea food is the order of the day. Large and busy in season.

LAGOS **Dom Sebastião**, Rua 25 Abril,20, Lagos.   Tel: 082 62795
Well regarded and reliable.
O Castelo, Rua 25 Abril,47, Lagos. Tel: 082 60957
English couple operate with experience and flair. Very good.
Alpendre, Rua Antonio Barbosa, 17, Lagos. Tel: 082 62705
Longstanding quality and reputation.

PORTIMÃO **A Casa da Jantar**, Rua de Santa Isabel, 14/16, Portimão. Tel: 082 22072.
A newcomer but fine food in good atmosphere.
A Lanterna, east over Portimão bridge, Parchal. Tel: 082 23948.
Established for excellent fish, duck. Superb.
O Buque, east over Portimão bridge, Parchal. Tel: 082 24678
Nautical decor with local dishes of fish, steak and duck.

CARVOEIRO/
LAGOA area

Centianes, Vale Centianes, Carvoeiro. Tel: 082 57724
Reputation for excellent 'Nouvelle Cuisine' but pricey.
O Leão, Porches. 8400 Lagoa. Tel: 082 52384
Fine reputation maintained by new ownership since 1984.

ALBUFEIRA

O Montinho, behind Hotel Montechoro, Albufeira. Tel: 082 53959
French cuisine and owned. Renowned.

SILVES

Rui, Rua Comendador Vilarinho,23/5, Silves. Tel: 082 42682
Well known for fine fish.

VILAMOURA,
ALMANCIL area

This area has an abundance of restaurants of all types and prices
Chinatown, Centro Comercial Miravila, Quarteira. Tel: 089 35498
Good authentic Chinese food in traditional decor.
Casa da Torre Ermitage, off Almancil/Vale do Lobo road. Tel: 089
94329.
Sophisticated international cuisine.
Sergios, Rua do Correio,30, Almancil. Tel: 089 95154
Friendly, bar/pub with excellent varied restaurant menu.
Chez Antoine, Estrada Quinta do Lago, Almancil.
Tel: 089 94428. French, intimate and good.
Belvedere, Vilar do Golf, Quinta do Lago, Almancil. Tel: 089 96615.
The golf course panorama adds to fine food.
Shepherds Casa Velha, Quinta do Lago, Almancil. Tel: 089 94541.
Fine reputation not always maintained.
A Floresta, Estrada Vale do Lobo, Almancil. Tel: 94588
Very popular good local cuisine at sensible prices.

LOULÉ area

O Avenida, Avenida José da Costa Mealha,13, 8100 Loulé. Tel: 089
62106.
Typical, good local food.
The Outside Inn, 4km from Loulé on Faro road. Tel: 089 90443
French cuisine, "Nouvelle style", but variety and portions.

FARO

Cidade Velha, Rua Domingos Guieiro,19 (Old city)Tel: 089 27145
Intimate old atmosphere with excellent reliable menu.
Lady Susan, Rua 1° Dezembro,28 Tel: 089 28857.
A good reputation close to shopping centre.
Monte do Casal, Cerro do Lobo,Estoi,8100 Faro.Tel: 089 91503.
Delightful setting and fine menu. (Estoi-Moncarapacho road)

Penina Golf
***** HOTEL

THE Penina Golf is situated in an oasis of peace at the centre of 3 magnificent golf courses designed by Henry Cotton. There is also a practice driving range and 2 putting greens Peninas private beach is just five minutes away by courtesy coach. The Penguin Village offers childrens swimming pool, childrens restaurant and many other facilities.

HOTEL DO GOLFE DA PENINA
Estrada Nacional, 125 Alvor, 8502 Portimão.
Tel: (82) 220 51/8. Telex: 57125. Fax: (82) 220 59.
General Manager Xavier F Rugeroni

Trusthouse Forte Hotels

Self Catering

Self catering in apartments and villas is very popular in the Algarve. There are a large selection of complexes offering a range of facilities many of which are covered by the Property Directory section of this book. The Portuguese National Tourist Office issues a Tour Operators' Guide which lists in detail all the operators to the Algarve with their specialities, addresses and telephone numbers. It also lists those who handle flights only but this information is also readily available from national newspapers. Travel agents will all have selections of brochures and in addition periodicals such as *Private Villas* which puts you in direct touch with owners of villas and apartments, available to rent.

Trusthouse Forte Hotels

Trusthouses have two hotels in the Algarve at present, the Dona Filipa, at Vale do Lobo and the Penina just west of Portimão. A third is under construction at Quinta do Lago and is to be known as the Hotel São Lourenço, located on a fine championship golf course of the same name also owned by Trusthouse Forte. It is anticipated to open at the end of 1990 and will have 150 rooms, a multitude of luxury facilities including pools and health club. Trusthouses intend it to be the finest hotel in the Algarve.

The existing **Dona Filipa** is a five star hotel adjacent to the Vale do Lobo golf course soon to be extended to 36 holes. It has full facilities including swimming pool, tennis courts restaurants and is also close to the beach.

The Hotel Golf da Penina is located on the fine championship course comprising 36 holes and designed by the late Henry Cotton. It has a five star rating and excellent facilities which include a large swimming pool, restaurant, grill room, games rooms, sauna and massage.

PART IV

LEISURE

Sports facilities

One of the promotion leaflets put out by the Tourist Board is entitled 'SPORTUGAL'. It is apt, as the Algarve is certainly a haven for enthusiasts of most sports. I will deal with them roughly in order of popularity.

GOLF Golf is the major sporting attraction of the Algarve particularly in the winter months, when many visitors from the colder and wetter climates of northern Europe come to play in the sun. Play is possible all the year round but it is perhaps too hot for some people in July and August.

At the present time there are eight golf courses in the Algarve with a further eight under construction and likely to be ready for play in 1990/1. Another seven have approval and should commence within a short period. Others are planned in principle and this increase should help to stabilise rising green fees, overcrowded courses and slow rounds, which are a commom feature particularly in the high golf season from November to March.

Mr Tony Barnabe, who is the golf professional at Vilamoura and a member of the Algarve Tourist Board, would like to see fifty more courses along the Algarve and it would seem that the present plans go some way to achieving that objective. All courses have teaching professionals and driving ranges.

Existing courses
1. Vale do Lobo - 27 holes.
2. Quinta do Lago - 36 holes.
3. São Lourenço - 18 holes.
4. Vilamoura 1 & 2 - 36 holes.
5. Penina - 36 holes.
6. Palmares - 18 holes.
7. Parque da Floresta - 18 holes.

Quinta do Lago golf course

Courses approved and under construction

1. Quinta do Lago
   New 18 holes commenced 1989.
2. Vilamoura - 27 holes open 1990.
3. Quarteira, Vila Sol - 18 holes open late 1990.
4. Pine Cliffs, Olhos d'Agua - 9 holes open late 1990.
5. Carvoeiro Club de Golf - 18 holes.
6. Jorge de Lagos Country Club, Carvoeiro - 9 holes open 1990.
7. Alto Club, Alvôr - 18 holes open 1990
8. Salgados, west of Albufeira - 18 holes.

Courses approved but not commenced

1. Vale do Lobo - additional 9 holes.
2. Silves Golf & Country Club 9 or 18 holes.
3. Porto de Lagos, Portimão - 27 holes.
4. Castro Marim (north) - 18 holes.
5. São Bartolomeu (Castro Marim) - 18 holes.
6. Conceição (Cabanas, Tavira) - 18 holes.
7. Ludo, Faro - 18 holes.

Courses planned in principle

1. Azinhal, Corte Velha - 18 holes.
2. Moinho Romeiras, Cerro da Corte,' Salir - 18 holes.
3. São Brás/Santa Bárbara - 18 holes.

Vale do Lobo
27 Holes. Par 36 (2 nines) & 35
Vale do Lobo, 8100 Loulé.
Tel: 089 94444
Telex: 56842 VLOBOC P

Quinta do Lago
36 holes. Par 36 each nine
Quinta do Lago, Almancil 8100, Loulé.
Tel: 089 94529 94782
Telex: GOLFOL P

Vale do Lobo   Designed by the late Henry Cotton, located on the Vale do Lobo complex, this is a tight course, famous for the 7th hole on the yellow nine across the ravine and cliff edge. Three loops of nine holes each is to be extended shortly to provide an additional nine holes. Villa development around the course has intruded and made it too narrow and 'trick' for the handicap golfer.

Quinta do Lago   Designed by the American golf architect, the late William Mitchell, and considered by many golf experts to be among the top ten courses in Europe. It is very picturesque, set in undulating terrain with pine trees and lakes creating some very interesting and testing holes. It is invariably in excellent condition, the tees and fairways being Bermuda grass and the greens are well watered, fast and true.

Quinta has hosted the Portuguese Open for the last few years and will no doubt do so again. It is a fine test of golf, not too difficult for the handicap golfer, and a delightful setting.

Another 18 holes is under construction and should be ready during 1990/1.

São Lourenço
Quinto do Lago
18 holes. Par 72.
Dona Filipa Hotel, Vale do
Lobo, 8100 Loulé
Tel: 089 94141

São Lourenço   This course was opened in 1988 and was designed by Joseph Lee and William Roquemore. It is owned by the Trusthouse Forte Group who are constructing the new five star, São Lourenço Hotel adjacent to the 18 green.

This course is full of challenging holes around the Ria Formosa estuary and lakes where the water is used to great effect. It is a fine course, perhaps too difficult for the longer handicap golfer, but as it matures it must rate on a par or better than the neighbouring Quinta do Lago. That is quite an accolade and it is epitomised by the superb 18th finishing hole around (or over for the brave), the large lake with a second shot to effectively, an island green.

Vilamoura One
8125 Quarteira.
18 holes. Par 73.
Tel: 089 33652/32321
Telex: 56914 LUGOLF P

Vilamoura One   Opened in 1969 and designed by Frank Pennink, this is a well established course which has hosted many tournaments including the Portuguese and Algarve Opens. It is reminiscent of some English courses, winding its narrow undulating fairways through pine trees with occasional views of the sea. The par threes are particularly difficult, especially the long sixth, downhill but often into wind. A very good test of golf!

Vilamoura Two
8125 Quarteira
18 holes. Par 72.
Tel: 089 35562/32321
Telex: 56914 LUGOLF P

Vilamoura Two   Opened in 1976 and originally called the Dom Pedro, it was designed by Frank Pennink but in 1985 altered and improved by Robert Trent Jones. The first nine holes are fairly open with fine sea views while the back nine winds through the umbrella pines. The well appointed clubhouse offers excellent food and the course, which is not too demanding, appeals to a broad cross section of golfers.

Penina
8500 Portimão:
18 & 9 hole courses. Pars
73: 35: 30
Tel: 082 22051/8
Telex: 573076 PENINA P.

Penina   The famous 18 hole championship course was designed by the late Henry Cotton and has hosted the Portuguese Open among many other tournaments. Originally carved from rice paddy fields, water in the form of lakes and streams plays an important feature. A flat but far from dull course, it has some fine holes, the par three 13th being perhaps the most memorable with a lake on the right which also guards the green. The Monchique nine hole course is across the road and reached by a tunnel, whilst a short nine with six par three holes, called the Quinta course, threads its way around the main course.

Palmares
Caixa Postal 74, 8600
Lagos.
18 holes. Par 71.
Tel: 082 62961/62953
Telex: 57434 PALMAR

Palmares   With superb views over Lagos, the bay and the Monchique hills, this course was designed by Frank Pennink and includes five holes over the sand dunes, links style, close to Meia Praia beach. It opened in 1975 and the tough par five 5th through the dunes needs three good shots to reach the green. Villas and apartments are to be built with full facilities including hotels on the adjoining land which hopefully will not spoil this attractive golf course.

Parque da Floresta
Vale do Poço, Budens 8650
Vila do Bispo.
Tel: 082 65333
Telex: 57173 GOLSAN P
Par 72.

Parque da Floresta   Set in a dramatic landscape this is the most recent course in the Algarve and was designed by the Spaniard Pepe Gancedo. It will need time to mature and perhaps some amendment before it achieves its potential. The excellent clubhouse serves good food and the surrounding development will include villas, hotel, pools, shops, tennis and squash.

TENNIS

After golf, tennis probably ranks as the next most popular participant sport. There are plenty of courts throughout the Algarve with a predominance in the central area. Courts are usually cement or a rubberised cement finish, not the all weather type. Below is a list of the better facilities available, although many more courts are under construction in new developments and are mentioned in the Property Directory. Professional coaching is available at the specific tennis centres and at the better class hotels and complexes.

East of Faro

Tavira Area
Pedras D'el Rei, Cabanas. Tel: 081 20281 - 6 courts.
Pedras d'el Rei, Santa Luzia. Tel: 081 22177/8 - 5 courts.
Eurotel, Quintas das Oliveiras, EN125 Tel: 22041/ 3- 2 courts.

Monte Gordo Area
Eurotel da Altura, Alagoa-Altura. Tel: 081 95450 - 2 courts.
Hotel Vasco da Gama, Monte Gordo. Tel: 081 44321/3 - 4 courts

Faro to Portimão

Vale do Lobo/ Almancil area
Roger Taylor Tennis Centre, Vale do Lobo. Tel: 089 94444 - 12 courts.
Hotel Dona Filipa, Vale do Lobo. Tel: 089 94141. - 3 courts.

Vilamoura area
Rock Garden Sports and Leisure Club, Caminho do Tenis, Vilamoura. Tel: 089 34740 - 4 courts.
Hotel Dom Pedro, Vilamoura. Tel: 089 35450 - 6 courts.
Hotel Atlantis, Vilamoura. Tel: 089 32535 - 3 courts.
Vilamoura Tenis, Vilamoura. Tel: 089 33899 - 12 courts (more)

Albufeira area   Hotel Alfamar, P.O Box 59, Praia da Falesia, Albufeira 8200 Tel: 089 50351/4 - 15 courts plus 3 indoor.
Hotel Montechoro, Albufeira. Tel: 089 53424/27 -10 courts.
Quinta da Balaia, Albufeira. Tel: 089 52512 - 5 courts.
Club Mediterranee da Balaia, Praia Maria Luisa, 8200 Albufeira. Tel: 089 52681/6 - 7 courts.

Armação de Pêra area   Vilalara, Praia de Redondo, 8300 Armação de Pêra. Tel: 089 32333 - 6 courts.
Vila Senhora da Rocha, 8300 Armação da Pêra. Tel: 089 32394 3 courts.

Carvoeiro area   Carvoeiro Club de Tenis, Carvoeiro. Tel: 082 57847 - 10 courts.
Quinta do Paraiso, Carvoeiro. Tel: 082 57248/57478 - 3 courts
Rocha Brava Tenis Club, Carvoeiro.Tel: 082 57775/9 - 4 courts.

Portimão area   Hotel Alvôr Praia (Hotel Delfim), Praia dos Três Irmãos, 8500 Portimão. Tel: 082 24021 - 6 courts.
Hotel Dom Joao II, Praia de Alvôr, 8500 Alvôr. Tel: 082 20135 - 2 courts.
Hotel Golf da Penina, Montes de Alvôr, 8500 Portimão. Tel: 082 53707 - 2 courts.

Lagos area and west   Luz Bay Club, Praia da Luz, 8600 Lagos. Tel: 082 69640 - 3 courts.
Ocean Club, Praia da Luz, 8600 Lagos. Tel: 082 69472/69763 - 5 courts.
Burgau Sports Centre, Fazenda da Amendoeira, Monte Novo. Tel: 082 65350 - 3 courts.
Hotel do Lagos, Rua Nova da Aldeia, 8600 Lagos. Tel: 082 62011 - 3 courts.
Hotel da Meia Praia, Meia Praia, 8600 Lagos.Tel: 082 62001- 2 courts.

SQUASH   Squash has increased in popularity in recent years and there is now a good selection of courts available. Below is a list of the better facilities available:

The following clubs have squash courts amongst other sports facilities:
Clube Barrington, Vale do Lobo, 8100. Tel: 089 94444. 5 courts (all glass back - 2 with spectator seating.)
Four Seasons Country Club, Quinta do Lago, 8106 Almancil. Tel: 089 94326 - 2 courts.
Rock Garden Sports and Leisure Club, Caminho do Tenis, Vilamoura. Tel: 089 34740 - 2 courts (near Golf One).

Burgau Sports Centre, Fazenda da Amendoeira, Monte Novo. Tel: 082 65350 - 3 courts (between Burgau & EN125).
Carvoeiro Clube, Praia da Carvoeiro. Tel: 082 57262/57266 - 2 courts.

Hotels & complexes with squash courts

Quinta da Balaia, Albufeira. Tel: 089 52512 - 2 courts.
Hotel Alfamar, P.O Box 59, Praia da Falesia, Albufeira 8201 Five covered and two open-air courts.
Vila Magna, Montechoro, 8200 Albufeira. Tel: 089 53611. 2 courts and club.
Hotel Montechoro, Montechoro, 8200 Albufeira. Tel: 089 53424/27. Four courts.

WATER SKI-ING This sport is not as readily available as one might expect due to the unpredictable sea conditions caused by the prevailing wind. It is certainly available in summer along the coast and at a couple of inland lakes although operators tend to come and go. Concessions are usually granted by the larger hotels and complexes on their own beaches and these are usually the most reliable.

The eastern coastline protected by the sand bars and islands is favoured and more protected but there are few operators.

Locations

Praia de Monte Gordo.
Vale do Lobo.
Vilamoura Marina.
Praia da Falesia - Aldeia da Acoteias.
Praia da Balaia & Praia de Albufeira.
Praia da Armação da Pêra.
Praia de Alvôr, Torralta
Meia Praia, Lagos.
Praia da Luz, Luz and Ocean Clubs.
Barragem do Arade, inland near Silves
Barragem da Bravura, inland from Lagos.

WINDSURFING Increasing in popularity and less susceptible to the sea conditions. It is available at nearly all the above locations for water ski-ing plus:
Cabanas, Tavira.
Santa Luzia, Tavira.
Quinta do Lago lake (with tuition).
Praia de Quarteira.

Water Slide Parks
Aquiline Water Park, EN125, Altura. (near Monte Gordo)
Atlantico, EN125, Quatro Estradas, Almancil, 8100 Loulé. Tel: 089 63757
The Big One, EN125, Alcantarilha. Tel: 082 32827 (north of Armação da Pêra)
Slide and Splash, EN125, Vale de Deus, Estombar, 8400 Lagoa. Tel: 082 53411/53421.

SAILING Apart from open sea locations there are protected lagoons along the coast at Faro, Olhão and Tavira. Inland situations on the Barragens Arade and Bravura are also available.

Sailing dinghies are available to hire at various places from most of the better hotels plus Carvoeiro Clube, Açoteias at Praia da Falesia, Luz Bay Club, Lagos Sailing Club, Torralta, Vale do Lobo and Vilamoura.

On a larger scale anchorage and harbour facilities are available at Vila Real, Olhão, Faro, Vilamoura, Portimão, Lagos, and Sagres.

The only purpose-built marina is at Vilamoura, and when the new extension is complete, there will be berths for 1,000 vessels, with full power, water and back up facilities. Chandlery, shops, restaurants, accommodation and the Nautical Club are all close at hand.

Vilamoura Marina, 8125 Quarteira. Tel: 089 32023 Telex: 56843

Other marinas are planned at Armação da Pêra for 600 berths and rumoured at Lagos and Portimão and on the Guadiana river near Vila Real.

FISHING Sea fishing either from the shore or from a boat is popular, whilst inland freshwater fishing is rare with few opportunities available. The Barragens do Arade, near Silves, and Bravura north of Lagos are freshwater reservoirs and fishing is permitted. The banks of the Guadiana, the border with Spain, provides an alternative location.

Sea fishing by boat can be arranged at a number of locations along the coast including Vila Real, Tavira, Olhão, Vilamoura, Albufeira, Armação da Pêra, Carvoeiro, Alvôr, Lagos and Sagres.

Shore fishing is popular with locals especially in the west at Sagres and Carrapateira. On the west facing coast the adjacent beaches at Arrifana and Monte dos Clerigos are considered very good. The best season is from October to February when moray eel, grey mullet, bream, bass and tope can all be caught.

HORSE RIDING This is a very popular pastime where the conditions and terrain are first class. The coast has a large selection of riding stables throughout its length, although there are fewer between Faro and Vila Real where the the terrain is less suitable. Horses available range from Arab thoroughbreds to children's ponies.

Some of the better stables are as follows:

Velha da Telha Riding Centre, Aljezur. Tel: 082 72174

Quinta dos Almarjões, Burgau. Tel: 082 65152

Torralta, (Aparthotel de Alvôr) Tel: 082 20111/32211

Hotel Alfamar, P.O Box 59, Praia da Falesia, Albufeira 8200 Tel: 089 50351/4 66351

Carvoeiro Clube, Praia da Carvoeiro. Tel: 082 57262/57266.

Solear Riding School, Porches. Tel: 082 52444

Quinta da Saudade, on Pêra/Albufeira road. Tel: 082 56182

Quinta da Balaia, Albufeira. Tel: 089 55787

Vilamoura Riding Centre. Tel: 089 66271 34377
Quinta dos Amigos, Almancil/Quarteira road. Tel: 089 95636
Horses Paradise, Almancil/Quinta do Lago. Tel: 089 96854
Pinetrees Riding Centre, Quinta do Lago. Tel: 089 94369

SCUBA DIVING

The Algarve coastline, mainly in the west, provides excellent snorkelling and scuba diving opportunities.

There is little organised diving, equipment or instruction available except at:
Clube Torpedo de Vilamoura. Tel: 089 35135
Aldeia das Açoteias, Tel: 089 50267

SHOOTING

Not a particularly active sport although some rough game shooting does take place in the hills north of the EN125.

However target and clay pigeon shooting is available at Vilamoura Shooting Club, located north west of the centre in the industrial zone. Tel: 089 33133

ATHLETICS

There are few facilities on hand but mention must be made of the fine track and field arrangements at:

| **Aldeia das Açoteias** |
| Apartado 34, 8200 |
| Albufeira. |
| Tel: 089 50267 |

Aldeia das Açoteias This complex which is close to Praia da Falesia and between Vilamoura and Albufeira, has extensive simple accommodation but is noted for its sporting facilities. These include 400 metre all weather track, pits for jumps, pole vault boxes, javelin approach, cross country track, tennis, and gymnasium. This is a well equipped training centre for serious athletes and has been used by many famous names.

Pure sports complexes and multi-sports clubs and facilities are rare but the following offer a good selection:

| **Clube Barrington** |
| Vale do Lobo, 8100. |
| Tel: 089 94444. |

Clube Barrington Squash, swimming (indoor and out), snooker and pool, table tennis, gymnasium, sauna, jacuzzi, steam room, golf range, putting green, bars, restaurants and accommodation. All equipped to a very high standard and membership is available on a daily, weekly and annual basis.

| **Rock Garden Sports and Leisure Club** |
| Caminho do Tenis, |
| Vilamoura. |
| Tel: 089 34740. |

Rock Garden Sports and Leisure Club Tennis, squash, five-a-side football, heated indoor pool, snooker, darts, cricket net, children's area, badminton, gymnasium, table tennis, card room, bar and restaurant with satellite TV. Full and temporary membership is available.

Burgau Sports Centre
Fazenda da Amendoeira,
Monte Novo.
Tel: 082 65350

Burgau Sports Centre   Tennis, squash, 5-a-side football, Kung Fu, gymnasium, volleyball, table tennis, snooker/pool, weight training.
Swimming pool, bar and TV, restaurant, sauna and self-catering bungalows.

FLYING   Light aircraft flying is available through the Aero Club of Faro based at the airport and at the Alvor airstrip near Penina.
Microlight flying is available at Vilamoura and Lagos airfields.

BOWLING GREENS   A sport on the increase with greens at Vale do Lobo, Vilamoura, Portimão and Praia d'Oura (Albufeira).

The Arts

THEATRE   The Lethes Theatre in Faro at the end of Rua Lethes was formerly a school founded by the Jesuits in the sixteenth century. It is an Italian style theatre of about 500 seats and is used for a variety of local cultural events, although there is no resident company.
Live theatre is rare commodity in the Algarve.

CINEMA   The following is a list of cinemas which show films in current circulation:
Vila Real de Santo Antonio   Cine Clube de V.R de S.A. Rua Teofilo Braga. Tel: 081 44537
Tavira   Cine-Teatro, Antonio Pinheiro, Rua Marcelino Franco, Tel: 081 22671
Olhão   Cinalgarve, Avenida da Republica, 176/180 Tel: 089 73332
Olhão   Cinema-Teatro, Rua das Lavadeiras, 5-a. Tel: 089 73153
Fuseta   Cinema Topázio, Avenida da Liberdade. Tel: 089 93384
Faro   Cinema Al-Garb, Rua Ataide Oliviera, 97. Tel: 089 28233
Faro   Cine-Teatro Farense, Rua de Santo Antonio 29. Tel: 089 22238
Vilamoura   in square opposite Casino. Tel: 33383
Montechord   Vila Magna Complex. Tel: 089 53611
Portimão   Cine-Teatro de Portimão, Largo do Dique. Tel: 082 23098
Portimão   Cine Esplanada, Avenida 3. Tel: 082 24484
Hotel Alvôr Praia   Alvôr. Tel: 082 24021
Silves   Cinema-Teatro de Silvense, Rua Dr. João Meneses. Tel: 42413

MUSIC **The Algarve International Music Festival**

This is an annual event which began in 1977 and commences in April and continues into June. In various locations throughout the region, it is a series of concerts, recitals, and performances including ballet with well known orchestras and performers.

The Algarve Folk Music and Dance Festival is held in early September at many locations. (See page 116).

FESTIVALS There are a multitude of festivals and fairs and the following is a list of the more important:

February 14-16th **Carnival, Loulé** Loulé is the centre of the traditional Carnival festivities for the Algarve, in the middle of the almond blossom season. Processions, floats and dancing all form part of this three day bonanza.

April 17th **Romaria da Senhora da Pideade, Loulé** Following the journey of 'Mãe Soberana', the Sovereign Mother on Easter Sunday to the town, the image is returned on this day in a great procession back to the shrine on top of Monte da Piedade, to the west of the town.

Estoi, Palm Sunday

May 1st **Festa do Primeiro de Maio, Alte** In this most attractive village the procession goes to the 'Fonte Grande' (large fountain), the symbol of life in a region which is short of water.

July 15-26th **Festa e Feira da Senhora do Carmo, Faro** On the 16th the procession of Our Lady of Carmel takes place but from the 12th there is also the Fair of Carmo, now an agricultural fair but with many other features.

August 14,15 **Festa e Feira da Senhora dos Martires, Castro Marim** An annual fair at which everything is sold and combines with the festival in honour of Our Lady of Martyrs in this old town dominated by the castle overlooking the town.

September 1st or 2nd weekend **Algarve Folk Music and Dance Festival** Over a three day period, sixteen different places hold various aspects of folklore, culminating in the Sunday evening when groups from all over gather at Praia da Rocha for traditional dance and song.

October 16th-23rd **Feira de Santa Iria, Faro** A traditional fair with many attractive features.

Outubro 26th-28th **Feira de Outubro, Monchique** A traditional fair attracting thousands and where you can buy almost anything including livestock and handicrafts.

Nightlife and Entertainment

CASINOS There are three casinos in the Algarve all under the same ownership, with a new one under construction at Vilamoura.

They all take the same format with a gambling section and separate entertainment facility which usually includes dining, dancing and cabaret.

Casino de Monte Gordo (on the sea front) Tel: 081 42224/5

Casino Vilamoura (in central area) Tel: 089 32919

Casino do Alvôr (next Penina Hotel on EN125). Tel: 082 23141/2

DISCOTHEQUES/ CLUBS

There is a good selection of discotheques/dancing clubs along the coast especially in the Albufeira, Vilamoura, Quarteira central area. The following is a selection:

Lagos
Lançarote Club, Rua Lançarote Freitas, 26 Lagos.Tel: 082 60890
Le Prive, Edificio Luz Mar, Praia da Luz. Tel: 082 69280

Carvoeiro
O Bote, Carvoeiro. (On the beach) Tel: 082 57285
Scott's Discotheque, Rua do Barranco. Tel: 082 57359

Guia
Atlantico, Guia. Tel: 089 56678

Portimão area
Horta II, Fontainhas, Mexilhoeira Grande. Tel: 082 96264
Lunatik Disco-Bar, Rua 25 de April, Ferragudo. Tel: 082 21137

Armação de Pêra
Discoteca Albatroz, Beco da Palmeira. Tel: 082 32951

Albufeira
Splash, Aparthotel Alfonso III, Albufeira. Tel: 089 55392
Kiss, Areias São João, Albufeira. Tel: 089 55639
Silver Screen, Avenida 25 de April. Albufeira Tel: 089 53447
Summertime, Vila Magna, Montechoro. Tel: 089 53611.
New York 1 (Açoteias) Tel: 089 66030

Vilamoura area
Mirage Club, Edificio Piramides, Vilamoura.
Skippers Disco Club, behind marina, Vilamoura.
Numero Um, Rua 25 de April, Quarteira. Tel: 089 33486
Trigonometria,Buganvilia Plaza,Quinta do Lago. Tel: 089 96751

Tavira area
Queen's, Pedras da Rainha, Cabanas. Tel: 081 20181

Monte Gordo
Discoteque/ Hotel Vasco da Gama, Monte Gordo. Tel: 081 44321
Discoteca Alcazar, Rua de Ceuta, Monte Gordo. Tel: 081 42184

CABARET ENTERTAINMENT

Many of the four and five star hotels have entertainment and dancing in house, especially during the high season.
Michaels Montechoro, adjoins Montechoro Hotel. Tel: 089 55997

PART V

THE GUIDE

This section takes the format of a conventional travel guide and includes relevant information on towns, villages, the coast, beaches, sites and buildings of importance and interest. Where appropriate cross references will refer to other sections of the book where additional information can be found.

Traditionally, the Algarve has been divided longitudinally into the Sotavento (the sheltered side) and the Barlavento (the windward side); the division falling roughly at Albufeira where the sandy beaches end and the cliff beaches begin. A central section was added by some experts but broadly the Sotavento has an eastern exposure and a lower screen of northern mountains, while the Barlavento has a maritime climate, cooler in summer and with greater exposure to the prevailing westerly wind and weather.

For your convenience it is divided into three sections: EAST, CENTRAL, and WEST.

EAST - **From Vila Real de Santo Antonio** (Spanish border) to **Faro.**

CENTRAL - From **Faro** to **Portimão.**

WEST - From **Portimão** to **Cape St Vincent.**

The Algarve is approximately 160 kilometres in length extending some forty kilometres inland from the coast. The main towns are the capital Faro, Tavira to the east, Albufeira, Portimão and Lagos to the west, all located on the coast. The relatively flat coastal plain extends inland between five and ten kilometres until it climbs into the two ranges of mountains, the Serra de Monchique and Serra de Caldeirão.

This is the Algarve and we begin in the east.

The East - Vila Real de Santo Antonio to Faro

This sector of the Algarve is the least developed of the three and for that reason is perhaps the most interesting presently and for the future. The topography and climate are different from the Central and Western Algarve. The countryside is quite lush with many pine *Fortress, Castro Marim* forested areas. It receives less rainfall and is warmer. There is less traffic and life is slower and more traditional. As a result there are fewer amenities and recreation. The beaches are excellent but often difficult to get to because of low lying marsh land. The coastline from Faro to Tavira is littered with islands and sand bars. This physical feature has meant that virtually no coastal development has occurred until you reach Cabanas, east of Tavira.

The eastern boundary is the River Guardiana and also the border with Spain. A new bridge is under construction just north of Vila Real de Santo Antonio which will replace the present slow ferry crossing to Ayamonte. This will generate traffic and enhance the tourism prospects of this end of the Algarve when it opens hopefully by 1992. This will link with a new freeway known as the Via Enfante running west as far as Lagos, but is not expected to be entirely finished by that date and will only go as far as Guia, north west of Albufeira. It will ultimately link with the new bridge over the River Arade at Portimão, which is currently under construction following a new section of road east between Lagoa and the river.

Physically this region is dominated by the Serra de Alcaria do Cume, a range of mountains rising over five hundred metres and stretching close on forty kilometres from east to west. It is a largely desolate and thinly populated area, crossed by only two roads of note. Roughly north to south the EN397/317 runs between Cachopo and Tavira and from east to west the EN124 runs from Alcoutim to Barranco Velho, the latter being the junction of five main roads. Both of these roads provide spectacular scenery and wonderful panoramic views (see Excursions section.)

Three rivers cross this range all eventually feeding the River Guadiana: the Foupana, the Odeleite and the Beliche. All three are an important source of water for this eastern region.

So we begin as if we had entered the Algarve from Mertola in the Alentejo on the EN122 and visit Alcoutim.

ALCOUTIM The most north easterly town in the Algarve and situated on the banks of the River Guadiana. A simple little town where narrow cobbled streets converge on the central square and lead on down to the church and the river. The church overlooking the river has plain white walls and a Renaissance portal.

Higher up, the castle on the hill faces the castle of São Lucas, across the river in Spain. The chapel of Nossa Senhora da Conceição looks across the sleepy town and the steps of the Manueline portico offer a place to rest, contemplate and view.

The square has a couple of cafes, a supermarket and even two

River Guadiana, Alcoutim

banks, showing that there is a real world out there! Be sure to cross the new bridge built in 1985 over the River de Cadavais. Pass the new school and turn right toward the river where a passable track, high up but alongside the river, provides delightful views up and down stream.

ODELEITE   Situated on the EN122 twenty kilometres north of Vila Real on the road to Alcoutim, it is simple to pass by and ignore. But venture down the very narrow streets, barely passable by car, to view the sheer simplicity of the place.

There are no buildings of special interest but the streets seem to fall away to the old church close to the edge of the river Odeleite, which crosses the main road higher up.

The prefix 'Ode-' is Moorish in origin common in the Algarve and loosely means 'water'.

MONTE FRANCISCO

Not a village really worthy of mention except that the bridge over the Guadiana, currently under construction, can be accessed from here. A raised, unmade, causeway style road leads east from the village through the low lying fen which extends to and around Castro Marim. This is part of the nature reserve of Castro Marim and some remarkable wildlife can be seen at close quarters.

CASTRO MARIM

Inland and a short distance away from the eastern Algarve's tourist centres lies Castro Marim, but a mere three kilometres from Vila Real on the EN122 at its junction with the EN125-6.

Steeped in history the town is dominated by two massive fortifications - the castle and the fort of São Sebastião - the latter on the highest hill in this predominately flat, marshy, landscape.

King João IV (1640-1656) built the fort of São Sebastião in the mid seventeenth century and it played a major part in the war of the Restoration (1644-1688). The view is superb with a fine window and arch framing the landscape, which stretches across the fen, the Guadiana river and to Ayamonte in Spain. The panorama is extensive. Below and to the north lie the town and Old Castle.

Archaeological findings confirm the presence of the Phoenicians, Greeks and Carthaginians before the Roman invasion and occupation by the Moors, the latter being finally conquered in 1242.

Henry the Navigator lived in the Old Castle in the fourteenth century and had a hand in building the church of São Tiago, which sits deep within the walls of the castle itself, having been restored after destruction in the 1755 earthquake. There are many other buildings within the castle, some recently converted into a museum where interesting finds can be seen from the archaeological dig which continues within the grounds.

The fine church of Senhora dos Martires sits close to the castle and has been well preserved. It features an unusual alcove on the southern wall with Manueline style capitals and a roof-wall with Christ's crosses, indicating that the reconstructor was a member of the order of Knights of Christ which succeeded the Order of Templars in 1321. This church is very important religiously in the area, giving its name to the annual festival and fair on 14th and 15th August.

There are many fine examples of typical Algarvian low built houses with roof-decorated walls showing an astute use of colour. The chapels of São Antonio and church of São Sebastião are also worthy of a visit.

Opposite: Senhora dos Martires

If ornithology and flora and fauna are your interests then this area

is indeed a special place. The fen of Castro Marim is a haven for migratory birds, an estimated one hundred different plants with a resistance to the dry climate, crustaceans and fish, all intermingled in this swampy aluvium land. More information and a guide is available from the Parks and Reservations Office in the castle.

VILA REAL DE SANTO ANTONIO

This town, near the mouth of the Guadiana river, was founded by the Marquês de Pombal in 1774 and is close to the site of the earlier town of Santo Antonio de Avenilha, which was destroyed by a tidal wave at the beginning of the seventeenth century.

Pombal, renowned for his organisation and rebuilding of Lisbon after the earthquake, created a symmetrical grid of streets; a central square for administration and religion, now named after him, and a broad avenue which runs parallel to the river facing Spain. His plans

Pombal Square, Vila Real de Santo Antonio

were extensive and he created the Company of Royal Fisheries, built a customs house, planted trees for shipbuilding and encouraged trade and industry.

However in 1774 Maria I, known as 'The Mad' banished the authoritarian Pombal and Vila Real went into decline until the end of the nineteenth century when tuna fishing reversed its fortunes. An Italian named Peroni started a tuna canning factory and latterly sardine canning added prosperity to the port.

It is a town with a short history and suffers from the endemic influences of being on the border with Spain. Traffic queues for the ferry to Ayamonte cause congestion on the Avenida da Republica and tourist shops abound in the centre in the streets around Praça Marquês da Pombal. Yet another change of fortune may be close with the opening of the new bridge to Spain in just a few years. The day trippers in both direction may change their habits.

Vila Real is connected to Monte Gordo by a pleasant road through a pine forest originally planted by the great Marquis. At night the lighthouse lights up the woods and dunes by the shore but by day provides panoramic views to Andalusia, Castro Marim and the mountains beyond. A new golf course is planned in this area.

MONTE GORDO

Three kilometres west of Vila Real and the most popular resort in the eastern Algarve, Monte Gordo offers long sandy and easily accessible beaches.

Once an important centre of the fishing industry (Henry the Navigator used to receive one tenth of the catch!), it became popular as a resort in the 1920s and in the 1930s boasted two casinos. On the east side the pine woods, referred to under Vila Real, reach down to the dunes and beach providing convenient shade and camping facilities. To the west the beach stretches for miles on to Praia Verde and Manta Rota.

There are now numerous hotels, aparthotels and self catering apartments both along the beach and in the town. The Hotel Vasco da Gama, perhaps the best known, occupies a prime position on the beach close to the casino. There are several restaurants and bars together with discotheques.

This is an ideal family holiday location with an abundance of facilities and Spain at hand for a day out and duty free shopping.

ALAGOA - ALTURA

Altura is the original small village on the main EN125 while Alagoa is the blossoming new resort on the coast. The latter has a new Hotel Altura designed for the package tour market and numerous small villas and apartments are being built. There is a small shopping centre with apartments above and a large complex called Alamar Village. This offers all the usual facilities: pools, restaurants, tennis and discotheque.

Growing demand is reflected by the recently constructed Waterslide park on the main road near Altura. Not an attractive area with much building activity, although the beach is excellent.

MANTA ROTA

A small beach resort village with little development to date. The houses, many with roof decorated walls, are of varying ages but a small village centre exists and a beach area with restaurant. There are some new apartments under way. The beach called Praia da Manta Rota is really an extension of Monte Gordo beach.

VILA NOVA DE CACELA

Cacela, now two places on the map, was, in the fourteenth century, a town of some importance and the centre of a district. They are now some two kilometres apart - Vila Nova being a pleasant spread out village off the main road and sporting the railway station. There are no notable buildings but there is a camping site in the hills to the north.

CACELA-A-VELHA

In 1240 King Sancho II won and lost Cacela from the Moors indicating its importance at that time. It was regained two years later and it is thought that the first church was built then, Cacela obtaining 'town' status in 1383.

The present church was built in the eighteenth century but retains a door in the north wall from the original. It has three naves and some fine interior pieces. The yard provides wonderful views across the ria and to the fortress next door. The fort, also built in the eighteenth century, is of no special interest except that it houses the Guarda Fiscal for obvious reasons!

The stillness and tranquillity to be found here and to be able to step back a century or two, makes it well worthy of the visit.

CONCEIÇÃO

This small village lies on the main EN125 north of Cabanas. A cluster of houses and a few shops hides the fine church of São Tiago, easy to drive by in a hurry, en route to Cabanas.

CABANAS

Sometimes known as Cabanas da Armação, it is a fishing hamlet but fast becoming a popular tourist spot. From Conceição after the railway line two tourist developments are located left and right. The one on the right is Pedras d'el Rei, a large sprawling complex of apartments and villas to rent. On the right is Quinta Velha, villas for sale and referred to in the Property Directory.

The village then spreads away from the main approach road in narrow lanes, until the promenade or front is reached. This does not directly overlook the sea, there being extensive islands and sand bars protecting the shoreline. Shops,even a small boutique centre, restaurants, apartments have all appeared along this front mainly to the eastern end. On private land at the far east end there is a fortress of St João built in the eighteenth century as protection against pirates.

To the western end lies Golden Club, again a tourist complex right on the beach and referred to under 'Accommodation'.

TAVIRA

Tourist Office: Town Hall,
Praca da Republica.
Tel: 081 22511
Post Code: P-8800
Population: 12,000.

River Gilhao, Tavira

A visit to the eastern Algarve would be incomplete without a visit to Tavira. It is my favourite town in the Algarve, although Silves and Lagos, which are quite different, run it close.

Historically, its foundation is thought to be about 2000 BC by the presence of the Turduli or the Greeks in 400 BC. To the Romans and Arabs it was important strategically and it finally became Portuguese in 1242 when conquered by Dom Paio Peres Correia as a revenge for the massacre of seven Christian knights by the Moors. It received a town charter in 1266, King João II lived at Tavira in 1489 and City

status was bestowed in 1520. A plague killed many inhabitants in 1645 and it suffered partial damage from the 1755 earthquake. The later silting up of the river estuary and the bar caused Tavira to lose some of its importance but the coming of tourism has revived its fortunes whilst farming, fishing and trade continue.

There is a lot to see and a good point to start is to cross the bridge and climb the hill to the castle walls, which command a fine view over a large part of the town. The most striking feature is the number of churches, thirty two altogether, many of which are in view. Also clearly visible are the steeper four sloped roofs, peculiar to Tavira.

The Castle   Only the walls in part are left and it was rebuilt by King D. Dinis in the thirteenth century. Other sections of the walls can be seen around the town, in particular the Arch of Misericordia at Rua da Galeria just off Praça da Republica. Next to the Castle is:

The Church of Santa Maria do Castelo   This was built on the site of a former mosque in the thirteenth century and is where King João I dubbed his sons knights after the conquest of Ceuta in North Africa. It was rebuilt after the earthquake and has a fine Gothic doorway with four small columns and plant designs on the capitals. There is an Arab window in the tower and the chancel has the tomb of Dom Paio Peres Correia and the seven knights killed by the Moors.

The Gothic and Manueline chapels have gilded and carved woodwork and there are eighteenth century tiles and some fine liturgical objects including a Baroque chalice.

The Church of São Tiago   This is situated just below the castle in a narrow street and has a distinct Moorish appearance.

The Church of Misericordia   An important sixteenth century church which has probably the finest Renaissance portico in the Algarve with the royal crown and city coat of arms. It stands out from the simple facade with Corinthian pilasters and in the cornice St Peter and St Paul keep watch over Senhora da Misericordia (Our Lady of Mercy).

It has three naves, capitals with gargoyles and an altar of carved and gilded woodwork. The eighteenth century blue and white tiles, depicting the fourteen works of mercy are very beautiful.

Back through the Arch of Misericordia into Praca Republica, also known as the Rossio of Tavira, the most imposing building is the.

Town Hall   An attractive building with mediaeval style arches. It includes some shops and the Tourist Office. A sculpted head at one end is said to be Dom Paio Peres Correia, the liberator of Tavira from the Moors.

Church of Misericordia, Tavira

Off the Praça are some fine houses and parallel with the river, a palm tree lined garden with a bandstand and cafes which leads to the market. Here you can buy fresh fish, fruit and vegetables plus a variety of other local goods.

Moving up the hill from the Praça along Rua de Liberdade on the left is:

The Chapel of Nossa Senhora da Consolação The altar here is sixteenth century and of the Flemish school and the tiles are seventeenth century. On up, bearing left, and on the Rua Tenente Couto lies the:

The Church of São José This adjoins and is the chapel for the hospital. It has Gothic and Manueline parts and a main door with rococco designs. Octagonal in design it has an interesting ceiling to the chancel with a barrel vault.

Church of São José, Tavira

Next to it is the tiny Chapel of São Brás with a Manueline vault (sixteenth century).

At an angle across a small garden facing the hospital is.

The Church and Monastery of São Francisco This has a distinctive high dome and and a gothic vestry. A large building in a high prominent position.

Bearing left here along Rua Poeta Isidoro Pires we reach the Campo dos Martires da Patria to find.

The Church and former Monastery of São Antonio There are three sculpted groups representing scenes from the life of the Saint and frescos above the main altar.

Church of São Sebastião is now a museum of paintings of the Saint's life.

Nearer to the River and in Rua Marcelino Franco is:

The Church of Nossa Senhora das Ondas Built in the reign of D. Manuel I and altered in the eighteenth century it has seafaring connections and is of trapezoidal design. The wooden ceilings have decorative paintings.

At this point cross the old bridge over the Gilão, which is Roman in origin but rebuilt in the seventeenth century, into the oriental quarter. On the main road out of town at the end of Praça 5th October is:

The Church of São Paulo This is seventeenth century in origin with a Renaissance style Galilee and portal with a bas relief of the Baptism of Jesus set high in the front facade. There are some fine fifteenth and sixteenth century paintings on wood. Nearer the river and in a square of the same name is:

The Chapel of Sant'Ana A modest simple exterior with a good view from the square and belvedere over the the river and town. High up in the Largo do Carmo overlooking the town is:

The Church of Carmo This eighteenth century church has remarkable carved woodwork and a Cupola with clerestory. There is a good view of the city from the adjoining former convent.

Tavira is well served by bars and restaurants especially on the south side of the River Gilão. Oddly, upstream above the bridge, it is called the River Sequa. Inland from Tavira the vineyards produce a good quality white wine which is an appropriate accompaniment to the variety of fish and shell-fish served in the local restaurants.

Carob and olive trees abound in the region and have grown here for centuries. As a result some huge specimens exist, some with perimeters of over seven metres and are between Tavira and Olhão and at Pedras d'el Rei.

LUZ   The main EN125 road passes through Luz and is joined by the roads from Santo Estevão and Moncarapacho. Entering Luz from the west the church strikes one immediately and was indeed the beginning of the village with its square and houses. It is considered to be one of the finest Renaissance examples in the Algarve. The huge main door with its unusual pediment dominates the facade. Above the door there is a niche where a statue of Senhora da Luz, carved in jasper, resides.

This remarkable lady with miraculous powers, and consequent attraction of pilgrims, is responsible for the growth of fine and typical houses with excellent roof-decorated walls. The houses in and around the church square are especially fine.

The side door of the church is a good example of the Manueline style but the belfry was built after the earthquake. The altar area has three seventeenth century canvasses.

Renaissance portel, Luz church

FUZETA A couple of kilometres off the main road, Fuseta is a very important fishing village. It is a smaller version of Olhão with similar terraced roofs and a Mosque-like domed church.

The port, well protected by sandbars and the islands of Tavira and Armona, is the focus of the village, the fish auction being the hub of commercial activity.

The church of Senhora da Conceição sits on top of the hill, its large yard commanding views across the productive ria. At low tide the women and children collect the shell fish which become exposed. Ferries are available to both the islands.

The railway winds through the village but little has changed here. Hopefully, it seems destined to remain a simple fishing village.

OLHAO The unattractive modern apartments on and around the main EN125 should not deter you from having a close look at this historic fishing town. It is the first town of consequence east of Faro.

It has a strange and intriguing history. Simple fishing huts existed in the middle ages but a solid stone house was not constructed until the early eighteenth century. The Moors left four hundred years earlier, yet the houses built around the the chapel of Senhora da Saudade with its mosque-like dome and the fishermens quarter of Barreta, are typically Moorish with roof terraces and intricate arabesque panels. Why this 'cubist' style of architecture should occur, reminiscent of paintings by Braque is hard to understand, other than the fact that the fishermen used to trade with North Africa. Nevertheless a walk through this quarter is a fascinating experience.

The port and large fishmarket make interesting visits and ferries can be taken here to the islands of Armona and Culatra, where long quiet beaches are available.

There are few buildings of historical importance except the parish church, with the chapel of Nossa Senhora dos Aflitos, especially for the women with relatives at sea. The chapel of Nossa Senhora da Saudade, referred to earlier, is next to the parish church.

The town's real claim to fame derives from 1808 when locals drove Napoleon's troops from the region and then a band of seventeen fishermen set sail for Rio de Janeiro to inform the exiled King João VI of the news. Thus Olhão achieved distinction and town status when the French were finally expelled in 1811.

MONCARAPACHO Moncarapacho, on the EN393 road eight kilometres from Olhão, is lined with vineyards which produce the wine for which Fuseta is renowned.

*Chapel of Santo Cristo,
Moncarapacho*

There are some fine examples of Algarve houses with squares with generally wider streets but the principal feature is the parish church with its superb Renaissance doorway.

Above the Ionic pilasters and the cornice are figures of St Peter and St Paul and further up again a niche of the Annunciation. There are three naves, Gothic signs in the high altar and the chapel of Senhor dos Passos. There are also fine seventeenth century tiles on several walls. The eighteenth century pulpit is unusual, being eight sided with paintings.

A short walk away is the chapel of Santo Cristo where there is a fine carved gilded wood altar, the ivory image of Santo Cristo to which miracles are attributed and the reputable pictures of Misericordia. Adjoining this chapel is a small but interesting local museum.

Climb up toward Cerro da Cabeça (249m) where there are fine views back to Tavira and Olhão. There are some interesting caves here created by underground water and streams.

QUELFES Quelfes lies four kilometres from Olhão and is an attractive and picturesque village. Vineyards and fig trees abound in this area either side of the main road. Some interesting streets lead to the church which has both Gothic, Manueline and Renaissance features.

ESTOI Estoi is north of Faro between Moncarapacho and Santa Bárbara de Nexe. It lies on a hillside at the foot of which is the church of São Martinho dating from the seventeenth century. It has a fine facade approached by steps, three naves and a tower with excellent views south.

Estoi Palace

Milreu ruins, Estoi

However the big attraction to Estoi is the palace of the viscounts, so called; an eighteenth century building of some stature with later additions, unfortunately in a state of disrepair. Entering through a side door past stables with an abundance of palm trees, a small bandstand takes one by surprise as the main house stands three levels above the formal and once elaborate gardens.

On a lower level there is a greenhouse housing sculptures of the Three Graces together with Venus and Diana. On the next level there is a lake and all around there are busts and statues of Emperors of Germany, King Carlos, Marquês de Pombal and many others. More busts and statues spread around the upper level where the palace on two floors overlooks the extensive grounds.

The palace has recently been acquired by the Faro local authority and it is planned to restore it to its former glory.

Milreu Roman ruins Situated a short distance west of Estoi one is immediately struck by the large church or temple-like building which indeed was used by Christians as a church and led some experts to think that this place was Ossonoba. Subsequent excavations have shown that Ossonobo was in fact sited at Faro and Milreu is believed to be a kind of weekend retreat or playground in Roman times.

The spa, considered to be fourth century, is in poor order but the overall ruins are interesting, although many items recovered now rest in the Museum Infante Dom Henrique in Faro.

SÃO BRÁS DE ALPORTEL

Located almost due north of Faro, about seventeen kilometres, São Brás is the heart of the Barrocal: the mid region between seaside and mountains and being calcareous, giving a vegetation of carob, olive and almond.

Although dating back to Arab and Roman times it was cork and the cork-oak trees that brought prosperity. The newer buildings in the north of the town indicate its commercial importance but south of the main Loulé to Vila Real road lie the low old houses with the distictive and typical 'acoteias' or roof terrace.

These narrow streets lead to the parish church and chapel of Senhor dos Passos (Our Lord bearing his cross). Some interesting vestments, gilded and carved woodwork and paintings make a visit worthwhile, apart from the fine view from the courtyard to the south.

FARO

Altitude: Sea level.
Population: 22,000.
Post Code: P-8000.
Telephone code: 00 89.
Tourist offices:Rua Ataide de Oliviera 100. Tel: 24067
Rua da Misericordia 8-12. Tel: 25404
Praca de Dom Francisco Gomes. Tel: 24753

Faro, capital of the Algarve since 1756, lies at the northern end of a lagoon, dotted with islands and salt pans. Arriving by air, these can be seen clearly at close quarters as the aircraft comes in to land. The airport, completed in 1968, is seven kilometres to the west of the town and has made Faro the focal point of the Algarve. It has enabled the tourist trade to grow rapidly and has caused Faro to lose some of its original character. The airport has been expanded and improved but has hardly kept pace with the annually increasing tourist influx. A large new terminal is under construction and should be open during 1989.

Faro has few modern buildings of any merit, but it has good shopping facilities (Rua de Santo Antonio), and reasonable hotels and restaurants. Many buildings of historic and of architectural interest were damaged or destroyed in the earthquake of 1755. Fortunately, however, several have survived or been restored, including the cathedral (thirteenth century), the Convent of Nossa Senhora and the church of S. Francisco (seventeenth century), all of which are situated within or close to the old walled city. There are other churches outside the walled town which are of interest and referred to later.

The harbour area of the town is colourful, the pavement cafes reflecting the relaxed atmosphere of the region. The harbour, apart from pleasure craft, handles local produce including wine, fruit, cork and fish. Walking towards the lagoons you may see storks and other bird life, especially in spring and autumn as migration takes place.

History

Faro, Moorish in origin, has been a settlement for over two thousand years. The ruins of a large Roman country house lie eight kilometres north of the town, near the small village of Milreu. This was, until recently, thought to be the site of the Roman town of Ossonoba, but now Faro itself claims this distinction after further Roman discoveries within the city itself.

Conquered by the Visigoths in 418, it became devoted to St Mary and was called Santa Maria de Ossonoba until occupied by the Arabs in 714 when it later became capital of the short lived principality founded by Ben Said Ben Harum in 1031.

A bishopric was established as early as the fourth century and subsequently liberated from Moorish domination in 1249 by Alfonso III. During the thirteenth to sixteenth centuries, through its connections with the royal families, Faro prospered, leading to city status in 1540 and to the transfer of the seat of the diocese in 1577, formerly at Silves. It had a large Jewish community, which is reputed to have established a printing press in the fifteenth century.

In 1596, during the period of Philip II's Spanish occupation, an English force, under the Earl of Essex, sacked and burnt the town. He looted a theological library of some 200 volumes, which belonged to Bishop Osorio, known as the *Portuguese Cicero*. Essex donated most of the books to the Bodleian Library at Oxford.

More serious damage to the town followed in the earthquakes of 1722 and 1755. Bishop Francisco Gomes de Avelar was primarily responsible for the extensive rebuilding, in the latter part of the eighteenth century.

In 1808 after occupation by Napoleon's forces commanded by Junot, Faro along with the other urban centres, rebelled and expelled the French invaders.

Sites

The modern part of Faro town has a complex one way street system, which repays study in advance if you plan to drive through it. The main area of interest, which is rewarding to walk round, lies within the charming and peaceful old walled city, located to the south-east of the harbour, off the southern end of the Praça de Dom Francisco Gomes. Enter through the interesting eighteenth century Arco da Vila. **Arco da Vila** (A tourist office adjoins). An archway that was formerly a castle gate, built in the eighteenth century by the bishop Dom Francisco de Avelar having Ionic columns and a niche with the

Faro cathedral

statue of St Thomas Aquinas. There is also an Arab portico within. The narrow Rua de Municipio leads to the stone cobbled, spacious Largo de Sé (Cathedral Square)

Cathedral or Sé   Possibly built on a Roman temple, a Visigoth church and having mosque characteristics, it is originally Gothic, built in 1251 and retaining the tower and two chapels from this era. A mixture of Gothic, Renaissance and Baroque it has a plain interior but the chapels of Nossa Senhoras da Conceição and Rosario are decorated with seventeenth century azulejos (hand painted tiles). Other chapels contain much decorative carved and gilded wood-work and inlaid marble. It contains the eighteenth century tomb of Bishop Pereira da Silva supported by two lions. There is a seventeenth century altar in the Sacristy and a gilt and red Chinoiserie organ, painted by Francisco Cordeiro in 1751.

Bishops Palace   Located across the square from the cathedral this is a splendid eighteenth century building, unfortunately not open to the public, and has some fine decorative tiles which can be seen in part through the doorway. A short walk across to the Praça Afonso III, brings you to the convent.

Convent of Nossa Senhora de Assunção This recently and beautifully restored convent building was founded in 1518-23 by Queen Leonora and has been converted into the Prince Henry Archaeological Museum. The main rooms surround a fine Renaissance two storey cloister and contain an important collection of Roman and pre-Roman remains. A Roman mosaic 30 feet long by 10 feet wide has been relaid in a room of its own. It was discovered in 1976, when a sewer was being constructed in Faro's Rua D. Henriques. Regrettably, the bulldozer operator shaved the beard of the handsome sea god! This find confirmed the view that the Roman town of Ossonaba was sited at Faro and not at Milreu.

Ferreira de Almeida Collection   The same convent building houses this exhibition of sacred and general paintings, curiosities and decorative objects. On leaving the museum and turning right, you reach the Arch of Rest.

Arco do Repouso (Arch of Rest)   Set within the old city walls and so called because King Alfonso III rested and later heard mass there after the conquest of the Moors. There is also a small eighteenth century chapel. Moving on across the impressive **Largo de São Francisco** to: **Church of São Francisco (seventeenth century)**   The interior is typically Portuguese with elaborate carved and gilded woodwork, azulejos, stone carvings and a picture of St Francis, ironically propping up a collapsing church, presumably during the earthquake.

Adjoining the hospital built in 1795 by order of Dom Francisco Gomes and on the Praça of the same name stands:

Church of Misericordia   Once a Manueline chapel only the portico remains. The church was rebuilt after the earthquake. Good examples of seventeenth century decorative tiles and gilded, carved woodwork.

Two museums are worth visiting.

Ramalho Ortigão Maritime Museum   Located in the same building as the Harbour Master's office, at the north-eastern end of the Praça de Dom Francisco Gomes, behind the Hotel Eva. Here the large variety of fish of the region are well depicted and a host of nautical nostalgia displayed.

Archaeological Museum, former Convent of Nossa Senora de Assunção

Regional Ethnographic Museum Located in the Rua de Portugal it has models of houses, chimneys, local costumes and crafts and a visit will provide an insight into local life and culture. There are also some large and impressive canvasses by the Faro artist Carlos Porfirio, a friend of Picasso.

North of the harbour area in the Largo do Carmo, the main Post Office faces the:

Igreja de Carmo (Carmelite church) This beautiful, twin towered, Baroque church was built in 1718 and is typical of the King D. João V period. Apart from the eighteenth century organ and carvings, there are paintings by Cristobal Gomez dating from 1595, but perhaps the most interesting, yet macabre feature, is the *Capela dos Ossos (Chapel of Bones)*

In the nineteenth century human skulls and bones were frequently used in construction and this chapel is considered to be a notable example of this practice. Just east of the Largo do Carmo lies the Largo de São Pedro:

Church of San Pedro Built in the sixteenth century it has a Renaissance portico, three naves with Doric columns. São Pedro is the fishermen's patron and there is some fine baroque carved woodwork, interesting paintings and a tiled panel on the right nave of the Virgin, St Michael and St Francis. In the same old district of the city near São Pedro stands:

Church of Santo Antonio dos Capuchos Not an impressive building but adjoining a monastery which was originally built in 1620, since restored and altered. The church does however house some fine glazed tiles. Secularised in 1910 it at one time housed the Archaeological Museum but now serves as the city mortuary.

Church of São Sebastião Thought to have been built in the fourteenth century, this small church has a Gothic chapel built of local limestone and spectacular blue and white azulejos either side of the altar.

In the northern part of the town behind the market stands:

Church of São Luis A small rustic chapel with unusual local architecture.

Beyond the far eastern end of the Avenue 5th October, high on a hill, 3 kilometres from the town, stands the tiny church of:

Santo Antonio do Alto Not of great architectural significance but the small museum adjoining devoted to St Anthony, is interesting with paintings, statues, engravings and books on St Anthony. It is also worth the journey for the fine panoramic views the hill affords over Faro town and the lagoon beyond from the adjoining tower.

Lethes Theatre   At the top of Rua do Lethes and housed in what was a Jesuit school converted in 1874 after a model of La Scala in Milan. The attractive result houses about 500 people with two circles and compact stage.

The Granary   North of the church of São Francisco and situated in what was the garden of the convent. It is small, hexagonal in shape and has bas reliefs representing mythological figures.

Church of Pé da Cruz   Rebuilt in the seventeenth century on what may have been the site of a synagogue. Interesting for the frescos on the walls and the outer chapel of Our Lord Distressed.

Palace of the Governors   Just outside Faro on the road to Portimão this very ruined and neglected building dates from the eighteenth century. A chapel in similar condition and secularised, adjoins.

Casa das Figuras   On the opposite side of the road to the Palace of Governors, this is a house or warehouse, possibly an outbuilding. The front has a large pediment in stone with strange figures of unknown origin but probably dating from the seventeenth century.

On a shopping expedition to the pedestrianised *Rua de Santo Antonio*, you will tread the black and white, patterned mosaic pavement. This type of pavement is quintessentially Portuguese. It will not be found elsewhere in Europe. The other stonework decoration, azulejo tiles, is also characteristically Portuguese and appears in churches and public buildings with great frequency.

Island of Faro and Beach   Only a short distance out of Faro and signposted off the airport road, it is reached by a causeway bridge across the Ria. It comprises a long thin sand island with two good beaches, one facing the Ria, ideal for water sports, the other the ocean.

There is a mix of old timber beach huts and more modern houses with a variety of restaurants, bars and open air cafes.

Ria Formosa or Ria de Faro   This protected region and nature reserve extends from the stream known as Ribeiro do Ludo to the Barra Nova at Olhão. It is an unusual group of navigable inlets between the coast and a series of low sand islands, created by the erosion of the sea and coastline. The main islands are Faro (beach), Barreto and Culatra, where fishing for rock bass, grey mullet, eel and a variety of shellfish, especially cockles, is popular.

The Ria also has a large number of salt pans which glisten white in the sun giving the area an attractive and unusual appearance. Bird life is especially interesting with some large species in evidence.

The Central Algarve - Faro to Ferragudo

THE COASTLINE

As we move west from Faro with the airport on the coast near Faro Island, the main EN125 forks left twice, first to Santa Bárbara de Nexe and secondly to Loulé. We will follow the coastline as far as Portimão and then look at the hinterland.

To the south of the main road lie the large estates and complexes of Vale do Lobo and Quinta do Lago where the long sandy beaches of Ancão and Garrão stretch as far as Quarteira. These complexes and the adjoining land are well documented in the Property Directory in Part 2 so refer to pages 56 and 63 for details.

Suffice it to say that they occupy some of the most valuable land in the Algarve and that residential property along this five kilometre stretch commands the highest prices. Fronting onto the western end of the protected Ria Formosa Nature Reserve, building is more carefully controlled. There is an abundance of golf courses at Quinta do Lago, Vale do Lobo and Vilamoura with more under construction and planned. Other sporting facilities such as tennis, squash, horse riding, water sports and sailing are all available.

QUARTEIRA

Tourist Office: Avenida Infante Sagres. Tel: 32217

This fishing village was known in Roman times and was still small until twenty years ago when tourism took over. Much has been spoken and written about Quarteira recently, none of it very complimentary. It does, however, demonstrate how indiscriminate, if not non-existent, planning and simple human greed can produce buildings with architecture that barely deserves the use of the terminology.

The old quarter around the church and fish market has almost vanished, whilst the eastern end is all new construction, mainly apartments and hotels. There are one or two decent restaurants in Quarteira and the fish market adjoining the general market is worthy of a visit to see the local catch. The Property Directory comments further on pages 00.

VILAMOURA

Adjoining Quarteira and separated only by the main road and football grounds, Vilamoura is in effect a new town. Laid out on 4,000 acres it is the concept of Arthur Cupertino de Miranda who formed Lusotur, the master landowning company in 1965.

Little has been omitted for the tourist and holidaymaker. Two 18 hole golf courses will soon be extended by a further 27 holes now under construction and the centrepiece is the magnificent marina also being extended to almost 2,000 berths. A new tennis club development is underway which will ultimately provide over forty courts. Most other sports are catered for including shooting, riding and squash.

Numerous villa and apartment developments have a wide range of facilities and there are hotels and aparthotels to suit all tastes. These are listed in the Property Directory in Part II and under 'Accommodation' in Part III.

Cerro da Vila   Indications of an earlier settlement and the natural harbour were discovered in 1963 when fragments of mosaic were turned up by an agricultural machine. Known as the Cerro da Vila, careful excavation has laid bare a Roman villa with wine cellar, a hexagonal shaped crematorium, a bathhouse and a smaller house,

Cerro da Vila, Vilamoura

probably servants quarters, revealing additional mosaics and many interesting objects. These are housed within a small museum categorised into Roman, Visigoth and Moorish and include pots, lamps, plates, glass, pins, bracelets, and necklaces.

Perhaps the most interesting items are three bronze age tombs remarkably preserved from about 1000 BC, clearly showing the skulls and bones of adults and babies in the foetal position.

These ruins are open to the public from 10am to 5pm daily and are well worth a visit. The elderly enthusiastic guide, in broken English, is very informative.

The central area has shopping facilities, a cinema and a casino with an abundance of restaurants throughout.The beach is the long sandy Praia da Falesia stretching about five kilometres to Olhos d'Água.

Vilamoura continues to develop and it will be some years before it is complete and a final judgement can be passed. Perhaps typical of such a large overall concept there has been a mixture of good and bad development and architecture. Time will be the ultimate judge.

OLOS D'ÁGUA

Another pretty little fishing village which planners and developers have tried hard to destroy. The tiny village harbour and beach now sports an array of bars and restaurants which somehow have failed to destroy the original character and charm. Large apartments and aparthotels built behind the village have brought tourism and prosperity.

There are freshwater springs in the sea which are very strong and mentioned by the Moors.

Between Olhos d'Água and Albufeira an enormous amount of development has taken place both on the coast and inland. At Balaia the luxury hotel has become a Club Mediterranee complex and Oura has seen an explosion of apartments, aparthotels and timeshare resorts. The latter are now recovering from the bad name created by using high pressure sales techniques. The better of these and various developments are listed in the Property Directory on pages 00

ALBUFEIRA

Post code: P-8200
Population: 8500
Telephone code: 089
Tourist Office: Rua 5
Outubro
Tel: 55428/52144

To see Albufeira properly it is best to park your car conveniently and go on foot through the narrow streets. Starting in the west, high on the hillside, there are excellent views across the town and coastline, sadly giving a clear picture of the extent of surrounding development. Moving down Rua Latino Coelho further vantage points emerge with access down to the beach. Then Peneco rock overlooks the beach with the same name but proceeding down the same street we reach:

The Church of São Sebastião   This church has a Renaissance portico and a Manueline side door. Stones brought from the old walls have been placed before the altar, some of which are Gothic. The dome above and roof structure has a Moroccan appearance.

The Chapel of Misericordia   Situated on Rua Henrique Calado the sixteenth century door and two adjoining windows appear to have survived the earthquake which almost completely devastated the town. This was probably built on the site of an old mosque and has a ribbed vault with the seal of the house of Avis between the Manueline decoration.

After passing the town hall, which looks like a church, lower down the Travessa da Bateria provides a good view over the fishermen's beach with its array of brightly painted boats. The old town behind it retains some ancient buildings and steps will take you down to the beach amongst the nets, pots and boats.

The centre of the beach is dominated by the Sol e Mar hotel with its tunnel below leading back to the main shopping street.

From the old town, steps inland will lead to the centre of the town. Although reconstructed after the earthquake there are some fine eighteenth century houses with stone doors and windows. The Praça Duarte Pacheco is the hub of activity for shops and produce, but undergoing drastic works, closing it to all traffic in March 1989. I trust the outcome will not spoil one of the more pleasant spots in Albufeira

Two other churches are worthy of visits: the **parish church on Rua da Igreja** and the **church of Sant' Ana** on Rua 1st December, both close together on the west side of the town.

At night Albufeira comes alive with a choice of bars, restaurants, discotheques and clubs.

Leaving Albufeira west the Xorino Grotto, an unusual rock formation is worth a visit, especially by boat.

São Rafael, Castelo, Galé   A series of interesting beaches extend west as far as Armacão de Pêra, the first being Baleeira, at the foot of a steep cliff, ideal for diving with calm water.

São Rafael follows, crescent shaped and well protected, then Praia do Castelo, a delightful place named after the rock formation. There are some pleasant walks across and under the cliffs to view the rocks, caves and scenery.

Praia da Galé then stretches away until it merges with Praia de Armação. Some development is taking place set back from these beaches but it appears to be of reasonable standard and is referred to in the Property Directory.

Opposite: Coastline near Galé

ARMAÇÃO DA PÊRA

Tourist Office: Avenida Marginal. Tel: 32145

Now a significant resort but originally it was the fishing village for the residents of Pêra, who appreciated the safety of fishing from there with the inbuilt protection of the fortress. Today the fortress on the east end of the front is the customs headquarters but also contains the small Chapel of São Antonio. Murals show scenes from the life of the Saint including his famous sermon to the fish, and there are two fine images of Patron and Senhora dos Aflitos. Below, the fishermen's beach is littered with boats and the fish is auctioned here.

Moving away from the fortress west the beach is interrupted by a projecting reef upon which sits a fine house, surrounded by palm trees, built at the turn of this century. Hotels and apartments line the avenue west and several massive projects are underway which seem totally out of keeping with the area. (See Property Directory page 77). Within the town are many restaurants, bars and discotheques. On the sea front are the Hotels Garbe and Levante; both well established and central. (See page 99).

On westward, Senhora da Rocha projects to sea, cut by tunnels and caves with the small pyramid topped chapel which is Romanasque, almost certainly pre-Moors. Immediately west are a series of caverns and grottos in the cliffs worth a visit by boat with names like Mesquita, Ruazes and the huge Pontal. The five star Hotel Levante is close, together with the luxurious complex at Vilalara. (See page 99).

CARVOEIRO

Tourist Office: Largo da Praia do Carvoeiro. Tel: 57328

Five kilometres south of Lagoa this once tiny fishing village has grown into a large holiday conurbation stretching four kilometres either side of the original beach, but still manages to retain some of its charm.

A vast number of villas and apartments have been built in the last ten or so years and it retains popularity despite the crowds in high season. The better schemes are listed in the Property Directory (pages 78-82).

Beaches are one of the attractions of Carvoeiro. Apart from the main village beach with a few fishing boats still operating, Centianes beach lies four kilometres east, small and sheltered: Carvalho (Smugglers Beach) approached through a tunnel in the rocks and Benagil, reached from the Lagoa to Carvoeiro road with a climb down – well worthwhile.

Whatever has happened to Carvoeiro over recent years in terms of indiscriminate development, the coastline has remained unchanged. This stretch is riddled with caves and grottoes seen to best advantage

*Church and point,
Senhora da Rocha*

from a boat. The best known is Algar Seco which is accessible from the cliff top and a fascinating shell encrusted rock formation.

There are now a multitude of restaurants and bars catering for all tastes and pockets.

FERRAGUDO Facing Portimão across the River Aráde this unspoilt fishing village retains its character despite some intrusion from tourism. The church on top of the hill is the highest point from where the white houses cascade down to the water's edge. A small square opposite the tiny bridge over a tributary is a centre of activity with bars and restaurants.

Out through the village the castle of St João Baptista, once in disrepair but adapted by the poet Coelho de Carvalho, stands overlooking the estuary and used by him as a home and literary hall.

On beyond lies the splendid wide Praia Grande and the lighthouse of Ponte do Altar with rugged and creviced cliffs to explore.

Central Hinterland - Santa Bárbara de Nexe to Silves

Moving west from Faro and the north of the EN125, taking the right fork at Patacão, we climb gently into the foothills of the Serra de Caldeirão towards Santa Bárbara de Nexe.

SANTA BÁRBARA DE NEXE

Situated just seven kilometres almost due north of Faro, this typical village has one of the most beautiful churches in the Algarve.

It is Gothic dating from the fifteenth century with three naves. It has some fine pointed arches, particularly the one leading to the chancel, which in turn has an intricate vaulted roof. There are also some excellent tiles along the aisles, in the vestry and above all in the triumphal arch where the patroness is depicted with two angels.

The tower of the church affords a good view across the fertile surrounding land which is rich in fruit and vegatables.

LOULÉ

Tourist Office: Edificio do Castelo.
Tel: 63900

This important town controls a large area including an important length of the coast from a local government point of view. The foundation is not known but the Romans were present and the castle is thought to have Moorish origins. It received a town charter in 1272.

The castle, or what is left of it, overlooks the Praça Alfonso III and is a good point to begin. It has been restored and the view from the towers gives some idea of its relationship with the surrounds. A modest museum and tourist office are within the walls together with a well which has a rim worn by ropes.

A walk along the adjoining narrow streets through the oldest part of the town, formerly the Almedina, will reveal local crafts such as wicker, copper and esparto and eventually lead to:

The Parish Church of São Clemente   The portal with pointed arches is thirteenth century and Gothic with unusual vegetable motif. Three naves inside have columns with splendid capitals and the chapel of All Souls has a Renaissance arch with seventeenth century tiles. There are some fine Gothic windows as well as Manueline vaults and arches. A mixture of styles, the tall belfry being the most recent addition.

Across from the church is Jardim dos Amuados, a park with hibiscus and palms within the churchyard with a good view south over the coast and the Shrine of Mãe Soberana.

Loulé market

The Church of Misericordia Situated on Avenida Marchal Pacheco this is now a health centre but the fine Manueline portal is sixteenth century and one of the oldest in the country. Opposite stands a granite cross with an image of the Virgin on its back.

A short distance up the hill on the same side a lane leads to Largo Tenente Cabeçadas and the portal of the Convent of Graça, the famed ruin of Loulé. The earthquake destroyed the convent and this is all that survived.

Back in the centre of town close to the Largo Gago Coutinho roundabout, the market functions every morning selling all manner of goods apart from the usual fruit, fish, meat and vegetables.

Praca da Republicana runs north west and contains the town hall and the old school. On the left a narrow lane contains the chapel of Nossa Senhora da Conceição. Of no significance externally, the tiny interior has some fine eighteenth century tiles and a beautiful image of the Lady.

The Church of São Francisco A simple exterior with a belfry of three bells and a Renaissance style dome gives way to the interior having a Baroque retable with images of the then patron and São Sebastião. It has eighteenth century tiles which add decoration.

The Shrine of Senhora da Piedade   Known throughout the Algarve as Mãe Soberana (Sovereign Mother) it was built in the early sixteenth century and the image dates from the same period. It lies almost due west of the town about one kilometre. The walls are covered with seventeenth century tiles and frescos represent the passion of Christ. Behind the church is a modern dome shaped cathedral in concrete which has never been completed. Spectacular views over Loulé, the Algarve and the mountains to the north are here to be enjoyed.

Loulé has some good shopping in and around Praça da Republicana, where local folk crafts are on view and there are several good shoe and leather shops.

Convent of Graça portal

ALMANCIL An uninspiring town ten kilometres west of Faro on the EN125 but with a new bypass opening later in 1989. This is very necessary as Almancil has become a traffic bottleneck due to its commercial success in various fields associated with the nearby developments.

There are some good shops and restaurants, estate agents and banks providing services to the wealthier tourists and residents to the south.

Two kilometres east of Almancil on the main road is the famous church of **São Lourenço**, a seventeenth century building with a dome. But it is the inside which has to be seen. The walls, the vault, even to the highest point of the dome are covered with superb tiles of blue and white. Panels depict the patron's life, The chancel has gilt

Church of São Lourenço

carving and the altar is made of local marble. This is an essential visit in this area.

Below the church there is an art gallery with some interesting modern paintings.

QUERENÇA Situated nine kilometres north of Loulé on top of a hill overlooking the valley. The main square and church are at the summit watching over the houses and streets that spread down the hillside.

The church has a Manueline portal but the tower was built later. The detail of the vault in the chancel is worthy of note as well as the baptistry, carved in stone with the image of Senhora da Assunção, patroness of the village.

Nearby the large cave of Salustreira is at points 36 feet high and full of stalactites. The Igrejinha dos Mouros, near Fountain Benemola has columns created by stalactites that reached the floor.

BOLIQUEME Just north of the EN125, this attractive white village has nothing special to offer but is a pleasant quiet place set on the side of a hill. The church is plain and simple with a belfry tower. In the chancel, São Sebastião watches from a throne.

The road to Paderne is winding and interesting for the changes of crop from fig to almond and olive.

PADERNE Some evidence of Moorish occupation is available here but little before. The original settlement perhaps called Badirna was on a high point south of the town. The ruins of a sandstone castle comprising walls and a tower can be found by taking a track to the left just before Cerca Velha and keeping bearing left. This deserted place with the stream in the valley below conjures up visions of the past. Within the walls there is what would appear to be the remains of a church but little else is known of this mysterious place.

In the town itself, half way up the hill, the church dates from the early sixteenth century and has Manueline characteristics in the chancel and facade. There is an eighteenth century image of Senhora do Castelo which legend has it, was saved from the chapel at the castle when the earthquake brought it to the ground.

BARRANCO VELHO An important meeting point of several roads in the foothills of the Serra do Caldeirão. The village is of no great significance but apart from the white houses, nearby there are some circular houses with stone walls and thatched roofs, similar to those found in Morocco. A small estate, part of the village, lies below the main road. It is accessible only on foot and is a cluster of old single storey houses which gives an interesting insight on the past and the people who are still living there among their chickens and animals.

SALIR Set on a ridge in the foothills of the Caldeirão it has the ruins of a castle of Arab origin at one end and a church at the other. Little but a tower and two walls remains of the castle but the churchyard has fine views south. An attractive unspoilt village.

ALTE Midway between Salir and São Bartolomeu de Messines, Alte is often said to be the most picturesque village in the Algarve. There are some fine views from the surrounding hills over the typical houses and streets.

The parish church of **Nossa Senhora da Assunção** is sixteenth century and has a Manueline portal. Inside it has eighteenth century tiles showing angels playing different musical instruments and the tiles in the chapel of Nossa Senhora de Lourdes are from Seville and sixteenth century. There is also a Manueline font. This is a very beautiful and special church.

There are also natural springs at Fonte Grande, and the Grotto of Soldos houses stalactites and stalagmites but is some distance and with difficult access.

Church of Nossa Senhora da Assunção

SÃO BARTOLOMEU DE MESSINES

Although there are no ancient monuments here, chronicles mention it in the conquest of Silves. It now lies in a valley just off the new main road, EN264 to Lisbon.

The church is sixteenth century but remodelled in the eighteenth century, having a Baroque entrance, columns like twisted rope and three naves. There are several chapels with decorative seventeenth century tiles and a pulpit made of coloured marble of the region. It is built mainly of local stone known as Silves stoneware. There are some excellent views from the roads in the hills that surround the town.

GUIA

Situated at a main crossroads on the EN125, it is perhaps now most famous for several restaurants which specialise in Chicken Piri-Piri. (Chicken grilled in a spicy chilli sauce).

It is a small village with narrow streets and has the church of Nossa da Senhora da Guia. It is eighteenth century and has some wood carvings and decorative tiles.

ALGÔZ

Set in a valley and an important junction of five roads. The landscape is attractive and windmills feature prominently. It still remains small and simple despite its importance for agriculture and trading.

The church is tucked away in a square and has some gilded carved woodwork and seventeenth century decorative tiles.

On a hill on the southern edge of the village is the Shrine of Nossa Senhora da Pilar with its white dome and excellent views from the yard.

PÊRA

A pretty village twenty kilometres south of Silves and just off the EN125. Here the inhabitants used to go to the seashore to fish and return afterwards to their homes. There are two churches, São Francisco under repair for some time and the parish church of the Holy Spirit. The latter has rococo wood carvings, sculptures of angels and a tiled panel representing the four Evangelists.

ALCANTARILHA

Lying just to the north of the EN125 this small town can be seen when approaching from both east and west as it sits in the valley of the river of the same name.

A restaurant and a bar or two mix with some fine and unusual houses as it slopes to the south. The parish church has a tall belfry and has been recently built but has some Manueline origins. The triumphal arch with twisted ropes and vault mark them clearly as sixteenth century. At the rear of the church there is a chapel of bones.

The whole chapel is constructed of skulls and bones with an altar of the same materials.

In the main street there is also the small nineteenth century chapel of Misericordia.

PORCHES Possibly occupied by the Romans, Porches has in modern times become synonymous with pottery making. A number of potters have gathered in this area and a regional style has been adapted with modern design to make this an interesting centre for the craft.

The parish church is nineteenth century on a sixteenth century site with the chancel of the original. A ribbed vault and and eighteenth century glazed tiles are interesting as is the fine view from the tower.

LAGOA Possibly a settlement on the edge of a lagoon, hence the name, since dried up, but in any event granted town charter status in 1773 by King D. Jose I. Now expanding and of considerable importance as a seat of local government, it has a prosperous wine industry through its Cooperative Winery producing a good white wine, an aperitif wine and a heavier red.

The nineteenth century parish church has a Baroque front and chancel with neo-classical portal. The Baroque chapel of the Santissimo has a beautiful image of Nossa Senhora da Luz by the eighteenth century sculptor Machado de Castro.

Lagoa church

Opposite the church are some pleasant gardens adjacent to which stands the town library, a nineteenth century building with an excellent portico and balustrade.

The church of Misericordia in the Praça da Republica is again Baroque with carved woodwork and excellent eighteenth century tiles. This square is the hub of Lagoa with the its busy market.

On the northern edge of the town in Largo Alves Rocados is the tower-belvedere, recently restored from the Convent of São José founded in 1713. On the ground floor there is the unusual 'Turn-box of the Unprotected' connected with the tradition of receiving abandoned babies at convents.

ESTÔMBAR

Estômbar is only three kilometres from Lagoa, ancient in origin with definite Arab connections as a river port. There are some fine old chimneys and it is an attractive village.

Estômbar was the home of the Arab poet Ibn Ammar and nineteenth century guerilla leader Remechido.

Parish church   Sixteenth century and Manueline having a façade with two symmetrical towers. Inside are three naves, unusual columns and eighteenth century tiles.

The Misericordia   One of the oldest and functioned as a hospital in 1531.

MEXILHOEIRA DA CARREGAÇÃO

The village by the river was founded by King Joao II in the fifteenth century. The grottoes of Ibn Ammar can be reached from the River Arade.

The chapel of St Anthony   is at the highest point in the village.

SILVES

Population: 10,000.
Altitude: 85m/280ft.
Post code: P-8300
Tourist Office: Rua 25
April,P-8300 Silves.
Tel: 42255

Silves lies 6.5km due north of Lagoa and the main E125. It can be approached on the N124 from Lagoa or on the N269 from Algôz and Alcantarila.

Each of these approaches takes you on a gradual climb through vineyards and citrus groves. The oranges grown in this area, around Silves, are considered to be the best in the Algarve.

The more scenic and dramatic route is from Lagoa and Algôz, where the roads converge south of the town. Over a summit, suddenly, the town sprawls across the north side of the valley: the white buildings climbing the hill from the River Aráde to the vast sandstone castle, the cathedral dwarfed alongside.

The old bridge, alongside the new, has six arches and was built in the fifteenth century using Roman methods. At the bottom of the hill, cross the new bridge over the Aráde and the town centre is ahead.

Silves cathedral

Silves today is a delightful quiet country town with narrow streets, shops and restaurants. Commercialism and tourism has had little impact and it is perhaps surprising that it has not been exploited. Until the sixteenth century it was comparable with Granada in terms of splendour and cultural influence. Already in decline, the earthquake of 1755 brought devastation. The castle and cathedral survived, although badly damaged.

Much of the culture and history of the Algarve is rooted here. Cilpes, as it was then called, existed in the fourth century BC with evidence of Roman occupation. It was, however, the Moors who established the town and made it great. They called it Xelb and it was their capital of the Al-Garb (Algarve) larger and more important than Lisbon.

In 1189 it was recaptured briefly by King D. Sancho I and had such significance that he called himself 'King of Portugal, Silves and the Algarve.' The mosque was consecrated and the diocese of Silves created, but only until the Moors conquered the town again in 1191.

It was the focal point of intellect and culture, finally becoming Portuguese for good, when reclaimed from the Moors by Afonso III in 1242. It became the See, seat of the Algarve's bishop, until transferred to Faro in 1580. This started its decline into insignificance, hastened by the almost total destruction caused by the earthquake of 1755.

The Moorish Castle   Restored in 1940, a massive red sandstone structure with battlements, it is entered through an imposing entrance gate. Ahead is an enormous bronze statue of Afonso III, who recaptured Silves from the Moors in the thirteenth century. A complete circuit of the battlements can be walked, providing superb views over the town roofscape and the surrounding countryside covered with citrus and forests of cork oak. In the courtyard, vast vaulted cisterns and ventilation shafts have been excavated which suggest that a fortification was in existence before the Moors.

A long flight of wide stone steps leads down from the castle. Half way down is the Cafe Ingles: a well known and pleasant restaurant for a meal or snack. Outside, tables overlook the Cathedral of Santa Maria.

Cathedral of Santa Maria   The thirteenth century cathedral, despite restoration, still has evidence of the earthquake damage, much of the original red sandstone having been repaired with stucco work. It has a fine doorway and the stone roof has been replaced by timber vaulting. A Moorish mosque is evident behind the altar.

Church of Misericordia   Situated opposite the Cathedral it has Manueline side portal and windows, having been rebuilt after the earthquake. The Manueline style of architecture was the climax of the late Gothic in Portugal, named after King Manuel I (1495-1521). It featured lavish surface decoration and elaborate structural members, in particular twisted columns.

Chapel of Nossa Senhora dos Martires   Situated in the lower part of the town with battlemented walls and built to the order of King D. Sancho I after the conquest of the town. Rebuilt after the earthquake, only the foundations remain and a Manueline vault in the chancel dates from the sixteenth century.

Cruz de Portugal   Sixteenth century in origin and about 10ft high it is located at the eastern end of the town on the EN124. It has figures of Christ on the cross on one side and descending on the other. It is sculpted from a limestone not found in these parts and is likely to have come from the north.

Following this same road (EN124) for 8km, turn left for the Barragem do Aráde. This dam and reservoir, set in the pine hills, collects the water for the irrigation of the area's profitable orchards. There is a pleasant restaurant and picnic area and water ski-ing and windsurfing are available on the reservoir.

Cruz de Portugal

The West Coast -
Portimão to Cape St Vincent

PORTIMÃO

Tourist Office: Largo 1°
Dezembro.
Tel: 082 22065/23695
Population 18,000.
Post code P-8500.
Telephone Code: 082

Firmly established on the west bank of the River Aráde, Portimão is the most important city on the Algarve from a commercial and industrial viewpoint. It established its prosperity and importance in the nineteenth century with the fish canning industry and became one of the main fishing ports. In 1924 Portimão became a city through one of its famous sons, the writer Manuel Teixeira Gomes, following his election as President of Portugal in 1923.

Unfortunately it is also perhaps the poorest in the Algarve for monuments, almost as if life started two hundred years ago after the earthquake. It is said with some diffidence that Phoenicians, Greeks and Carthaginians were attracted to the natural harbour but there is little doubt about Roman presence, who called it Portus Hanibali or Portus Magnus.

In 1250 it is thought to have been recovered from the Moors by the Knight of the Order of St James at the same time as Silves, Alvôr, Estômbar and Porches. It became a town in 1453 and was attacked by Moors, Dutch, English and Spanish forces in the sixteenth and

Portimão harbour

seventeenth centuries, which brought about the construction of the fortresses at São João, Ferragudo and Santa Caterina, Praia da Rocha. The 1755 earthquake removed most of the evidence of earlier history.

The Parish Church   Originally constructed in the fourteenth century in Gothic style, its reconstruction has retained the Gothic portal within a high portal with decorations resembling flames rising skywards. The right tower is very prominent and can be seen from most parts of the town. Inside there are some fine seventeenth century tiles and walnut carvings. There is a fine image of St Peter in white marble and a cross brought from the Convent of Esperança. This convent is on the road to Praia da Rocha and is now a fish factory, a Manueline fifteenth century building in ruins!

The Church of the Jesuit College   Situated in the Praça da Republicana facing the market. With only one nave this large church has a severe façade which has probably been altered. There are three carved altars against the far wall. Above the middle altar is a marble niche with the image of Senhor dos Aflitos. On the party wall with the school there is a sixteenth century door which probably came from another chapel.

There are some attractive seventeenth century houses in the centre of the town, on or near the main squares with beautiful tiles and wrought iron balustrades. The gardens and cafes near the river are a meeting place and the fishing boats with their catches are always a source of interest. Grilled sardines in one of the quay-side cafes is an experience special to Portimão. Shopping facilities are good with a large and comprehensive market in Praça da Republicana and a tiled pedestrian shopping street close by at Rua do Comércio. Rua Santa Isabel nearer the bridge has shops specialising in local handicrafts, art, crystal and leather.

The tourist influx has caused congestion problems in Portimão resulting in serious traffic jams over the bridge, particularly in the high season. This problem will be eased in the near future with the construction of a new bridge over the river Aráde upstream, and causing through traffic to bypass the town completely. It is underway and due to open early in 1991.

PRAIA DA ROCHA   Now in effect the tourist resort for Portimão, it grew up between 1930 and 1950 when British writers and intellectuals stayed. It was known as a resort before the tourist boom of the Sixties and is very cosmopolitan.

The **Fortress of Santa Catarina de Ribamar** was built in the sixteenth century to defend Portimão. Inside is a small chapel with a Gothic doorway. There is also a pleasant cafe and there are some excellent views across the estuary.

Avenida Tomás Cabreira follows the rugged coastline west to Três Castelos and Vau and is lined with hotels and apartment blocks. Below the rocks and seashore there is a fascinating spectacle of caves, caverns, inlets and tunnels which can be explored or viewed from cliff or beach. This stretch is cut by João de Arem Point on the west of which lies Três Irmãos where the rock formations continue, creating small accessible sand beaches and caves.

The development now being extended at Prainha, overlooks the cliffs followed by the Hotels Alvor Praia and Delfim at Três Irmãos. The massive development at Torralta then cannot be ignored, a plethora of high rise apartment blocks finally giving way to the old fishing village of Alvôr.

ALVÔR

Twice destroyed, first by the Crusaders in 1189 and then by the earthquake of 1755, Alvôr remains a narrow maze of Moorish type streets and alleys. The houses are low and simple.

The Parish Church Rebuilt after the earthquake this lovely Manueline building houses the large image of the Crucified (Senhor dos Navigantes) which was rescued from a grounded ship. The portal of this church is superb, carved in local stone, richly decorated with figures and ornaments, yet retaining a simplicity. Its location is also splendid, both high and low tides giving different aspects.

The Chapel of São João provides lovely views from its position covering the estuary and the bay from Lagos to João de Arem Point.

ODEÁXERE

Surrounded by rice fields this pretty village has a parish church with a Manueline portico in red sandstone from Silves, together with some good seventeenth century tiles.

LAGOS

Tourist Office: Largo
Marquês de Pombal.
Tel: 082 57728
Post Code: P-8600.
Population 10,000.

The presence of the Phoenicians, Greeks and Carthaginians is certain and the Romans later called it Lacobriga: 'laco' meaning lake and 'briga', fortified. The Romans were present from fourth century BC followed by the Visigoths in the fifth century AD. The Moors arrived in the eighth century and destroyed much of the town.

The walls and the town fell to King Sancho I in 1189 along with Silves and Alvôr. They were soon lost again to the Moors and not recovered finally until the reign of King Afonso III.

Henry the Navigator lived and died here. The famous sailor and Henry's pupil, Gil Eanes was born here and was the first to sail around Cape Bojador in West Africa, returning to Lagos with a barrel for Henry containing earth and roses from Africa.

The walls of Lagos indicate effectively how large it was in the time of King Sebastião when he proclaimed it a city and capital of the Algarve, at the end of the sixteenth century.

The lower part of the town, now dominated by the Avenida dos Descobrimentos, was once regularly under water and it was not until 1960 that this road, with the attendant sea reinforcements, was built. The town hall which is nineteenth century, until then had waves breaking against it, the post office and law courts having been built since that date.

We begin in Rua da São Gonçalo where we find:

Church of Santo Antonio   Located in Rua de São Gonçalo it is dedicated to the army regiment that was once stationed here. It is a superb example of gilded wood carving internally, while the outside is by contrast, relatively simple. The wall at the back of the chancel is maybe pre-1755 and the side walls have six pictures of the saint performing miracles which are exceptional examples of eighteenth century Baroque.

There is a statue of St Anthony and another of St Eloi with unusual dress.

Municipal Museum   This adjoins the church of Santo Antonio and has a number of interesting exhibits. After a room of archaeological items there are displays of typical Algarvian crafts, African items, paintings and a room dedicated to Lagos which has some very valuable pieces. There is also a fine coin collection and finally a section of sacred art in which the garments used for the mass before the battle of Alcácer-Quibir are displayed.

Church of Santa Maria or Misericordia   A sixteenth century building situated close to the museum and church of Santo Antonio in Praca da Republica. It was restored after a fire in the nineteenth century but has an original Renaissance main door. A recent fresco in the chancel is part of interior renovation and there are some valuable images of Nossa Senhora da Piedade and São Gonçalo de Lagos. A large area of ornate plasterwork from the nave vaulted ceiling had unfortunately just fallen prior to my visit.

The Slave Market   This is on the corner of Praça da Republica and comprises a group of semi-circular arches and columns which is considered to be the first market for slave trading built in Portugal.

Coastline near Lagos

The slaves came on the Caravels from Senegal and Guinea. A walk through the streets of the centre, many of which are pedestrianised, is interesting with a wide variety of restaurants, banks and shops. Focal points are at Praça Gil Eanes and Praça Luis Camões and not far from the latter we come to:

Church of São Sebastião Situated in the upper, northern part of the town and known to have existed as early as 1325. The side door portal is Renaissance and in 1490 the Bishop of the Algarve had the chancel built in honour of São Sebastião, who was made patron saint of the town for having saved it from a serious plague.

The naves are lined with Doric columns and there is some fine carved, but not elaborate woodwork. The tower gives excellent views all around. There are also some fine images including one of Our Lady of Glory which is over two metres high and reputedly taken from a wrecked vessel. A crude crucifix is believed to have been at the battle of Alcácer-Quibir. Seventeenth and eighteenth century tiles are impressive as well as a small charnel house at the rear.

The Walls   The existing structures were built in the reigns of Manuel I and João III (sixteenth century) on earlier bases. Apart from the obvious stretches along the seashore , there are long sections with defensive bulwarks, inland behind the town.

Church of the Carmo (Nun's church)   Now in ruins but at the rear of the town in Largo da Vasco Gacias, this interior has some interesting features including carved woodwork, tombstones and decorative tiles.

Fort Ponta da Bandeira   Built to defend the city in the seventeenth century. Restored recently with its ditch and drawbridge.

Chapel of São João   Situated outside the walls close to Rua Infante de Sagres, it is thought to be possibly mediaeval in origin having been restored in the seventeenth and eighteenth centuries. It has an eight sided chancel and gilded and carved woodwork. It is in a bad state of repair.

The Beaches and Coastline of Lagos   Lagos is richly endowed with superb sandy beaches and remarkable eroded cliffs and rocks. North of the city and harbour lie São Roque and Meia Praia, with long stretches of sand to the Alvôr estuary.

Batata and Pinhão are small rocky cove beaches close to the centre and fortress and accessible by steps. Next is Praia Dona Ana, much developed around with hotels and apartments, but still a delight to approach from the cliff top.

Camilo, with very difficult access follows, but the cliff edge route here to Ponta da Piedade is magical with an incredible array of colour – red and ochre shades predominating – in the rock formations and hues of blue in the sea. The shapes carved by water and wind erosion are awesome with the earthquake of 1755 playing its part in cutting off the rock from the mainland where a shrine once stood on Ponta da Piedade. All that remains is the stub of a column.

Caves and grottoes abound and boat trips along this coast can be obtained from both Batata and Dona Ana beaches. A boat trip adds another dimension to this fascinating coastline.

Canavial is another small cove followed by Porto de Mos, the first long beach since Meia Praia and where some major development is to take place.

PRAIA DA LUZ This looks like a recent tourist creation but in fact there is evidence of Roman occupation. It has been an established fishing village where whales were once caught. The remains of a small eighteenth century fortress guarded it against pirates.

The church, of no great importance, has a rebuilt tower, for which the locals collected the funds, the original having been destroyed by a hurricane in 1941.

Now firmly established as a popular resort and dominated by the Luz Bay Club and the Ocean Club, (See Property Directory) both of which provide good accommodation with full sporting and entertainment facilities. The beach is wide and sandy and is separated from Porto de Mos by the steep rock cliff of Atalaia.

BURGAU The village centre lies at a cross roads high above the beach and the narrow streets slope down steeply. Tourism has made some impact but the charm still remains and the physical geography should prevent a mass invasion and leave it as a quiet, attractive, unsophisticated place.

SALEMA On west from Burgau, and for the adventurous with the appropriate vehicle, Salema is approachable along the coastline on rough bumpy tracks via some delightful coves, particularly Boca do Rio. Alternatively and more sensibly it is approached by the road south from the EN125 between Budens and Figueira.

Tourism has made its mark here with a camping site north of the village, apartments and the Beach Club set back from the beach. Fishing still survives on a pleasant and deep sandy beach and the pretty original village street, very narrow, climbs away parallel to the coast and eastward.

The Beaches between Salema and Cape St Vincent

Turning off the EN125 to the south at Raposeira there are beautiful beaches at **Ingina** and **Zavial**. Both are unspoilt with only a few villas in the valley approaches. Zavial is the larger but both have small restaurants and are worthy of the detour from the main road. Further beaches but with difficult access are at Barranco and João Vaz.

Moving on west and close to Sagres, a turning left off the main road takes you to **Praia do Martinhal**. Here there is a pleasant motel, with a large development planned and the beach is wide and spacious with dunes and small islands out at sea. From Martinhal, Sagres is in view with its fishing port and beach of Baleeira. An active fleet can be seen here with a fish auction close to the beach.

The Points of Baleeira and Atalaia project to sea, to the west of which is the beach of Mareta, longer than Baleeira and extending to the town and Point Sagres.

To the west of Sagres, steps lead down to the tiny beach of **Tonel**. This is difficult to access and a little risky when the wind blows hard, a common occurrence!

Between Sagres and the Cape lies **Beliche**. The seventeenth century fortress has been restored and the chapel dedicated to Sta. Catarina may have been on the site of a convent. Here there is convenient cliff top parking and an easy path to the long beach. It is, however, exposed to the westerly wind.

SAGRES AND THE CAPES

Tourist Office: Municipio
Tel: 64125.
Population: 1500
Post Code: P-8650.
Telephone Code: 082

West of Lagos, the Algarve dramatically changes character. The protection of the Serras, de Monchique and do Caldeirão, from the fierce Atlantic winds and weather, vanishes. The flora becomes sparse, the olive, fig and almond trees hide in the valleys leading to the rocky beaches and coves.

Europe's most south-westerly extremity has its own theatre and history. Until the end of the fifteenth century it was undoubtedly 'World's End'. One man did not believe the theory and his name, Infante Dom Henrique (1394-1460), known as Henry the Navigator, dominates this area.

Compass Rose, Sagres

History

Cape St Vincent is far better known to the British than the more southerly facing and adjoining Cape Sagres, primarily due to the famous naval battles fought off this coast against France at the end of the eighteenth and early part of the nineteenth centuries. Cape Sagres has, perhaps, had a greater impact on history, certainly Portuguese history, than its famous neighbour.

Henry the Navigator was the son of King John of Avis and Phillipa of Lancaster, the daughter of John of Gaunt and therefore half English. When not in Lagos or Alcobaça, he spent a large part of his life at Cape Sagres and died here in 1460. Hard evidence of his work on navigation is scarce but he undoubtedly laid a foundation that resulted in voyages of discovery during his lifetime and after his death. Henry became Grand Master of the Order of Christ, formerly the Knights Templar, and borrowed heavily from this order and the Abbey of Alcobaça to finance his expeditions. His nephew, Afonso V, continued Henry's work after his death, despite the debts.

Henry sponsored the Caravel, the first ship to sail across the wind. This put Portugal ahead of the world and enabled Henry to begin to achieve his ambitions which were summarised by the chronicler Azurara:

'First; to explore the lands beyond the Canary Isles; second, to find if there were Christian people in Africa with whom to trade; third, to discover the extent of the Moors territories (assess the enemy);

169

fourth, to find a Christian kingdom to help win the war against the Moors; and finally, to extend the Holy Faith.'

Columbus was without doubt one of the select few chosen by Henry to realise these dreams. They differed in approach, in that Columbus believed in a due west route to the riches of the Indies, whereas his mentor was convinced of the existence of a route round the bottom of Africa, then east.

After Henry's death, the later voyages of Bartolomeu Dias round the Cape of Good Hope in 1488 and of Vasco da Gama to India and back in 1498-9, confirmed Henry's view. Columbus, sailing in the Spanish service, succeeded in reaching the West Indies in 1492. Cabral, who discovered Brazil in 1500 and Magellan who circled the globe in 1520, all owed a debt to this remarkable and farsighted prince.

Sites

Sagres is a small harbour town, spread across a windswept rocky plateau. **The Ponta de Sagres**, a promontory projecting in to the sea, was known to the Romans as the **Promontorium Sacrum**. It is here, according to the legend, that the body of the martyred St Vincent was brought ashore in the eighth century. Subsequently, so the legend tells, guarded by ravens which flew along the route, the remains were remarkably transported to Lisbon in 1173!

Now a state-run pousada, the **Vila do Infante**, claims to have been the site of the home of Henry the Navigator, from where he founded his famous school of navigation. These facts are disputed and were not assisted by Sir Francis Drake's sacking of the town in 1597. Portugal was, of course, under Spanish rule at the time. Further damage was caused by the earthquake of 1755 and only the adjoining fifteenth century chapel survives.

A large bleak fortress, originally sixteenth century but rebuilt after the earthquake, contains the giant **Compass Rose**: stones set out in the form of a compass, said to have been used by Prince Henry to train his student seamen.

The Gothic fifteenth century church of Nossa Senhora da Graça nearby has a door from a later period but the image of Sta. Catarina inside is known to have been in Henry's chapel.

Sagres has a good selection of sea food restaurants, two good hotels and the state run pousada.

The windy, exposed road from Sagres to Cape St Vincent passes through Fort Beliche and arrives at the rocky headland, 200 feet above the sea. The ruins of the sixteenth century monastery adjoin

Cape St Vincent

the lighthouse and the climb up the spiral staircase to the observation platform provides a fitting climax to an excursion to this historic area.

Looking west and allowing the imagination some freedom, it is not difficult to visualise the many historic naval encounters that have taken place in these often storm-tossed waters. Drake, who occupied the Capes in 1583, regularly raided Philip II of Spain's fleet, as it returned from South America with treasure, to prepare his Armada in Lisbon or Cadiz. Sir George Rook was defeated by Admiral Tourville in 1693 and Rodney attacked a Spanish fleet in 1780. Admirals Jervis and Nelson, with fifteen vessels, defeated twenty-seven Spanish men-of-war in 1797.

It is estimated that some two hundred ships a day pass Cape St Vincent and the lighthouse's powerful 3,000 watt beam is visible sixty miles away. A variety of ships can usually be seen, but on my last visit to this desolate place it was shrouded in fog. The echoing fog horn from the lighthouse added another eerie dimension to this dramatic land and seascape.

The Western Hinterland

Going due north from Portimão the EN124 leads to Porto de Lagos where the road forks left to Monchique becoming the EN266, following the valley of the river Boina.

This road climbs into the hills through forests of eucalyptus interrupted by views of the river where peasants can still be seen washing their clothes. First we reach:

CALDAS DE MONCHIQUE Just four miles south of Monchique itself, this famous spa town dates back to the Romans with its remedial waters. The Moors used it and King João II (1495) came to cure 'dropsy' from which he suffered. There are five springs gushing vast quantities of water some of which is now bottled for drinking. Reputedly the waters cure rheumatism, respiratory and digestive ailments.

The town square has a pleasant twentieth-century atmosphere and there are some fine walks around with excellent vistas south to the coast.

MONCHIQUE Apart from King João II, King Sebastian visited here in the sixteenth century and in 1773 Monchique became a town. Wood crafts and the making of barrels and casks is traditional and its popularity as an attractive and healthy place to live has increased.

The Parish Church   This is a sixteenth century Manueline style building of some size. The portal has a pointed arch and a Manueline rope fixed by five rosettes. Inside, the columns made of the local Foia rock, are eight sided with capitals like thick ropes. The chapel of the Blessed Sacrament, on the left, is pre-earthquake and has a vault with two crossed arches. The patroness of Monchique, Senhora da Conceição, is represented by a fine image from the eighteenth century. There is some fine carved woodwork and decorative tiles. Further up the Rua do Porto Fundo we come to:

The Church of Misericordia   This eighteenth century church, recently restored and having a Baroque altar has a carved wooden pulpit and some interesting paintings. Higher up the same hill we reach:

The Shrine of Senhor dos Passos   This is a small building in a rural Baroque style with two belfries and contains the image carried through the village over Lent, a life size figure of Christ.

The Convent of Nossa Senhora do Desterro   This is a Francis-

Monchique

can convent in ruins. Only a façade and nave remain but at the rear it has the famous Fonte dos Passarinhos (little bird's fountain) with a surround of decorative tiles. The convent farm has walnut and plane trees as well as a huge magnolia. The views are exceptional. Some interesting tours are close at hand:

Picota is a peak at 2,320 feet with superb views of the coast and inland lies Monchique in the valley and the hills beyond.

From the centre of Monchique and the Largo 5th of October the road to Foia is away to the south west. The change in vegetation is soon noticeable and as the trees disappear the terrain becomes rugged and the bushes and scrub lower. Foia is the highest point in the Algarve at 2,730 feet and the view is a complete circle. If it is not too hot and not wet, the views are spectacular, as far as Faro south east and Arrabida, near Lisbon, to the north.

South from Monchique, Pé da Cruz houses a number of folk craft shops where blankets, baskets and wooden items can be purchased. On through Meia-Viana and Nave, a large quarry will show you what 'foiaite', the local rock looks like. The road continues through a cultivated and sheltered valley until you reach:

MARMELETE An uneven up and down village where the parish church sits in the centre and the shrine of São Antonio at the other end. So far away from the tourist intrusions this place remains untouched and unspoilt.

Another route north west to Foz do Farelo up the northern slope of Foia provides superb views especially across the bridge of Mata-Porcos.

ALFERCE which is six kilometres up the EN267 from Pé da Cruz is a picturesque village with a parish church and findings here indicate traces of a pre-historic fortification. There are also some typical Algarvian rural houses.

Back on the EN125 west of Portimão, the road due north towards Monchique takes you through:

ALCALAR On the side of the road to the left and easily missed is a neolithic necropolis. It comprises burial holes in the ground where skulls and objects have been found such as pottery and ornaments which are kept in the museum in Lagos. Other finds suggest Iron Age burials which makes them three thousand six hundred years old.

Moving north on the same road, again easy to miss but set in woods to the right and opposite a cafe of the same name is:

The Chapel of Senhora de Verde   Literally meaning Lady of the Green, a poetic name for the Virgin, it is a ruin by a stream with a Manueline portico. It is a delightful spot and legend has it that the Lady appeared on the bank of the stream hence the miracles and cures associated. Back on the main EN125 above the valley of the Odeáxere river lies:

MEXILHOEIRA GRANDE This village is surrounded by farming land irrigated by the Bravura Dam. It is a mixture of new houses and typical Algarvian dwellings.

The parish church, restored a century ago, is Renaissance with a Manueline side portico and tower. On west on the EN125 and south of the river of the same name sits:

ODEÁXERE Surrounded by rice fields, this pretty village has a parish church with a Manueline portico in red sandstone from Silves, together with some good seventeenth century tiles. Some eight kilometres north west of Lagos on the EN120 through Portelas you reach:

Chapel of Senhora de Verde, Alcalar

BENSAFRIM A typical village of some size which has spread along the roadside. Turn into the narrow streets and see the quiet older parts including the church of São Bartolomeu with its belfry and interesting ceiling.

Bravura Dam Returning on the road to Lagos turn left at the signpost to Colinas Verdes and bear left again to the dam. This is wild and rugged terrain until after about four kilometres the Bravura Dam appears. Water sports are available here and a road runs some way round the lake. From Bensafrim the road west passes through:

BARÃO DE SÃO JOÃO A small village of single storey houses with a church having twin towers. Some houses here are colour-washed making a pleasant change from the standard white. Back on the main EN125 the next town is:

BUDENS   The small village groups around the parish church which has some fine liturgical objects and vestments, the latter thought to date from the sixteenth and seventeenth centuries and of oriental origin.

Across the road the chapel or shrine of St. Lawrence has a Moorish appearance and some seventeenth century decorative tiles. About three kilometres west of the village of Figueira do not miss :

The Chapel of Nossa Senhora da Guadaloupe   This is a superb example of Roman-Gothic and built in the thirteenth century, possibly by the Knights Templar. It is thought that Henry the Navigator worshipped here. The single nave has a chancel with a cross-ribbed vaulted ceiling but the most interesting feature is the sculpted capitals of several human faces, remarkably lifelike for the period.

RAPOSEIRA   Only a kilometre from Vila do Bispo, this attractive little village groups round the parish church. Prince Henry may have lived here but little ancient evidence remains apart from the odd Gothic doorway.

The Chapel of Nossa Senhora da Encarnação   This church has a Manueline doorway and side chapels of gilded and carved woodwork. There is a statue of Our Lady of the Incarnation, probably sixteenth century.

VILA DO BISPO   Known as the Granary of the Algarve and formerly as Santa Maria do Cabo. It received town status in 1663 after its Bishop, Dom Fernando Coutinho, donated it to the Cathedral at Faro, hence its name, literally, Bishop's Town.

The town is spread out over a small hill. The parish church is worthy of note having some fine blue and white eighteenth century *azulejos* covering the walls of the chancel. A good example of rural Baroque, the high altar is in gilded and carved woodwork. A vaulted ceiling over the altar is decorated with the Virgin and Child in blue. A small museum displays artefacts, prayer books and ecclesiastical robes.

There are also some simple and beautiful houses all built after the earthquake, which was particularly severe in this area, being very near the epicentre. It is said that only one house survived. Behind the town are some pleasant windmills with wrought iron weathercocks.

Torre da Aspa, six kilometres west of Vila do Bispo, provides splendid views from a height of just over 500 feet south across the whole of St. Vincent and Sagres area.

The road north from Vila do Bispo, the EN286, goes through rugged wild terrain with small lakes by the roadside. There are numerous small beaches on this west facing coastline, some of which are accessible by car such as Castelejo, Cordoarma and Barriga.

After Carrapateira, with a good hotel and restaurant (see Accommodation) you come to the small village of :

BORDEIRA
Originally a military garrison in the eleventh century, little survived the earthquake except a barn with a sixteenth century niche. Close to the barn is the simple church rebuilt several times but with a Manueline doorway, taken from the ruined Manor House. Some twenty kilometres further north lies Aljezur.

ALJEZUR
Spread across three hills with the Castle dominating one, the layout of the town is interesting with the streets following the hill contours and the tall buildings so placed near the brook so as not to obscure the views of others.

Aljezur

Occupied by the Arabs in the tenth century, the castle was conquered in 1246 by the Master of the Order of St James, Dom Paio Peres Correia, liberator of Tavira, and King D. Dinis granted town charter in 1280.

The Parish Church Built in the nineteenth century at the wish of the bishop Dom Francisco Gomes de Avelar, in order to avoid the plague of mosquitoes near the brook, and to encourage the town in that direction. The original village remained, creating a divided town. There is a fine statue of Our Lady Of Dawn and a gothic chalice.
The Church of Misericordia Built in the sixteenth century and rebuilt in the eighteenth century it has a simple Renaissance portal.
The Castle Affords excellent views of the town but ruined by the earthquake. The water tank remains, a reminder that Aljezur was the last stronghold to be recovered from the Moors.

In the Largo 5th Outubro stands a reconstructed sixteenth century Pillory, a punishment place from the past.

ODEÁXERE Close to the Alentejo this attractive village is on a slope running down to a stream. It has a beach four kilometres away into which the stream runs, through the fertile valley, cultivated alongside. A quite unspoilt village, with the stream being the border between Algarve and Alentejo.

Odeáxere

PART VI

EXCURSIONS

The following are suggestions for days out to places of interest. Full details are available in the main guide section in Part V to all the places mentioned. They start from various points but can be combined, reversed or joined at any place of convenience.

FROM FARO AREA **East from Faro**

Take the EN125 east to Olhão, a fishing port where ferries can be taken to the islands of Armona and Culatra. Continue east turning off the EN125 to Fuzeta, an unspoilt fishing village. Return to the E125 via Luz, with its superb church and on to Tavira. Tavira is worthy of plenty of time, perhaps a separate visit and is a most attractive town. Back on the EN125 take the EN270 via Santa Catarina to São Brás, a delightful drive through lovely country. São Brás is a mixture of old and new with fine views from the churchyard south. Return to Faro on the EN2.

A shorter trip east and north

Again east to Olhão but turning inland on the EN398 to Moncarapacho, a fascinating, quiet old town with a beautiful Renaissance church and local museum. Now head west out of Moncarapacho, crossing the EN398 and make for Estoi. Here you have the famous Palace, a fine church and just east of the town the Roman ruins at Milreu. All are worthy of your attention. The EN2 will take you back to Faro or alternatively continue west to Santa Barbara de Nexe, another pretty village with a fine church.

A longer trip inland covering the Eastern Algarve

This is a full day out but takes you through magnificent scenery and covers a large section of the eastern Algarve. Head away from Faro to Loulé on the EN125 and 125-4. Loulé has a lot to offer and is worthy of a separate visit. North east from Loulé on the EN396 lies Querença, just off the road and worth a brief look at the church. At the sharp T-junction with the EN124, turn right and on to Barranco Velho, an intersection of four main roads. The EN 124 takes you deep into the hills and on to Cachopo where another world appears to exist, like

Martim Longo with its stork's nest perched on top of the church belfry. The EN124 crosses the EN122 and you quickly arrive at Alcoutim on the River Guadiana. A castle, two churches and some fine views of the river are worthy of note before heading south via the EN122.

This road takes you through some scenic undulating country via Odeleite and Azinhal, little villages which the big world has left alone. At Monte Francisco across the fen, the new bridge from Spain is under construction (May 1989) and the link roads to the EN125 and the new Via Infante will no doubt change this area.

Soon the castles at Castro Marim appear on the skyline and these are worthy of your attention as indeed is the surrounding fen if you are interested in bird, marine and plantlife. A short drive takes you to Vila Real de Santo Antonio, the creation of the great Marquês de Pombal. Here you can cross by ferry to Ayamonte in Spain or continue west through the pine forest to Monte Gordo, a modern tourist town complete with casino. The main road will return you to Faro but the sandy beaches along the stretch to Tavira are quiet. Cacela Velha and Cabanas are worthy of a visit.

FROM ALMANCIL, VILAMOURA, ALBUFEIRA AREA

A trip inland

From the EN125 turn off to Boliqueme, which has a pleasant atmosphere and church. Follow the EN270 to Paderne and if inclined turn off left on to narrow tracks just before Cerca Velha and follow the occasional signs to 'Castelo'. Patience will reward you with a splendid sight!

From Paderne follow the EN270 until it meets the EN124 and turn right to Alte, often described as the typical Algarve village. Grottoes, streams and fountains add to the attraction of this town, now showing signs of commercialism.

Retrace your route on the EN124 and make for São Bartolomeu de Messines, with its unusual church façade. On the same road directed to Silves, the Barragem do Aráde lies off to the right, a spectacular artificial dam.

Silves has a lot to offer: a Moorish castle, a cathedral and narrow streets with interesting shops and restaurants. South on the EN124-1 takes you through orange groves and vineyards to Lagoa, the parish church, old convent under restoration, and market, all of interest. Back on the EN125 going east, Porches, a centre for pottery, Alcantarila and Guia, the place for Chicken Piri-Piri, are all on your way back.

FROM PORTIMÃO, CARVOEIRO, ALVÔR AREA

Inland to Monchique

Two routes, one directly north on the EN124 from Portimão or via Lagoa and Silves can be taken – the latter avoids crossing Portimão bridge if approaching from the east. The roads join at Porto de Lagos and follow the valley of the Arade, upstream. Climbing steadily you reach Caldas de Monchique, the famous spa town with its old world charm. On up to Monchique, set on the hill side with two interesting churches and higher up a ruined but fascinating ruined Franciscan convent. There a lots of folk-art shops and the road climbs on higher to Foia, the highest point in the Algarve with spectacular views to the coast, provided the weather is clear. There are plenty of restaurants to choose from where *chicken piri-piri* and *presunte* or smoked ham are the specialities of the region.

FROM LAGOS AREA

Go north out of Lagos on the EN120 towards Bensafrim. A fork right will take you on an interesting diversion via Cotifo to the Barragem do Bravura, a dam and lake where fishing and water sports are available. Bensafrim is a quiet little place but the EN120 climbs on, eventually joined by the EN268, ultimately reaching Aljezur, an historic town with a castle and two churches. On north, the most north west town in the Algarve is Odeceixe on a hillside with a stream running to a beautiful beach.

Retracing the route, bear right at the junction between the EN120 and 268 and you will come to Bordeira, now a small village but in the eleventh century a military garrison. This stretch has many fine beaches, some of which are accessible by car. Vila do Bispo is known as the Granary of the Algarve, and is an important junction. The main road continues south to Sagres and west to Cape St Vincent, all well documented in the guide. The EN268 and 125 will return you to Lagos via Raposiera and Budens, but don't miss the tiny, historic church of Nossa Senhora de Guadaloupe on the left side of the road between these towns.

SHOWER SYSTEMS

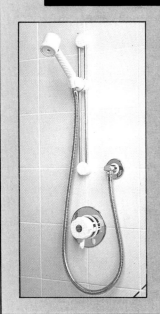

Aqualisa thermostatic and manual shower systems give a really high performance from a standard gravity fed, combination boiler, gas multipoint or balanced high pressure supply. The secret lies in the unique design of the valve and shower head which allows a flow comparable to pressurised showers. Add to this an accurate blend of hot and cold water to a constant temperature of + 1°C, automatic safety cut out should the water supply fail and in-built descaling features and it is no surprise that Aqualisa is one of the UK's most popular domestic showers.

Flexible or fixed head models are available. Choose chromium plated, light (incalux) or dark (incaloy) gold with either black or white.

PUMPED SHOWERS

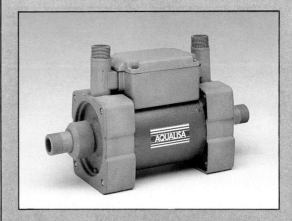

Where insufficient head is available to provide a high flow rate, (eg. apartment installations, loft conversions etc), then you will be glad of the Aqualisa fractional HP twin-ended pump. It has been specially designed to guarantee compatibility with Aqualisa thermostatic valves and the high output showerhead and will provide up to 3 ½ gallons of temperature controlled water every minute even in a negative head situation.

Four of the best from
AQUALISA

AQUAMIXA

For over bath shower installations the new thermostatically controlled Aquamixa is the perfect answer. It is a high flow rate shower combined with bath filler that plumbs directly into the bath feeds and locates in the tap holes provided on all baths conforming to British Standard specifications. It is therefore ideal for commercial use, particularly hotels, and for refurbishment projects since no alterations to existing plumbing or structure are necessary. Models are available for gravity fed, multipoint/gas combination boiler, or balanced high pressure systems.

The Aquamixa range also includes basin taps and monobloc and bidet monobloc. Available in chrome, dark (incalux) or pale (incaloy) gold and white.

TURBOSTREAM

A combined gravity and pumped shower system offering a choice of flow patterns – standard, pulsating, high powered needle or aerated spa. The power mode is operated by a touch button which instantly activates a pneumatic switch on the pump which means there are no electrics and, unlike many powered showers no complicated wiring. Like all Aqualisa shower systems, Turbostream is controlled by the unique thermostatic valve to provide perfect control to + 1°C and perfect safety. Available with fixed or flexible hose shower heads and in gold or chrome and white finish.

Agent for Portugal: Brian Nuttall,
Stroudwater Park,
St. Georges Avenue
Weybridge, Surrey, KT13 0DT.
Tel: 0932 840496.

Also a
Apt. 317, 810(
Almanci
Algarve
Tel: 089 9620

PART VII

APPENDIX OF INFORMATION

Services Directory

The following is intended as a useful list of contacts which is believed to be correct at the time of going to print.

Portuguese Chamber of Commerce & Industry in the UK

4th floor, New Bond Street House, 1/5 New Bond Street, London W1Y 9PE Tel: 01 493 9973 Telex: 918089

Airlines telephone reservations

T.A.P. London 01 828 0262   Manchester 061 499 2161
British Airways 01 897 4000
Dan Air 0293 820222   Charter 01 930 2782

Surveyors

Property Consultants International Limited.
Chartered Surveyors, P.O. Box 209, 8106 Almancil.
Tel: 089 97745/65   Telex: 58877 PCIL   Fax: 97781
Robert S Levitt FRICS ACIArb. John A Bradstreet FRICS

Architects

Architects Design Management, EN125 Almancil 8100, Loulé P O Box 138
Tel 089 95332
Les Pustelnik

G. I. Architects and Designers, Edificio Lela Letra F 3.0.
Tel: 089 97351.
London Office: Thames Wharf Studios, Studio 8 Rainville Road, London W6 9HA.
Tel: 01 381 8652/8690   Telex: 936295 GIARCH
Fax: 01 385 9934.
Gabriella L Inglesias RIBA - Principal.

Atelier do Sul, Esplanada de Santa Maria, 8100 Boliqueime.
Tel: 089 66123/66402/66479   Telex: 56040
Fax: 089 66439
Architecture, Publicity and Printing.

Design and Build Packages

These companies will find land, design houses and build and manage the project to completion. They are also government licensed agents:-

Goodfellow Smith Lda. Apartado 240, Correio Central, 8000 Faro.
Tel: 089 90166   Telex: 56771 MEDRON P.

Giebels Propriedades Lda., Estrada National 125, São Lourenço, 8100 Almancil.
Tel: 089 95353
Telex: 56704 GIEBEL P

Financial Services

The Bachmann Group, P.O. Box 175, Frances House, Sir William Place, St Peter Port, Guernsey, Channel Islands.
Tel: 0481 23573   Telex: 4191637 BACFID F.
Bachmann Overseas Ltd., EN 125, Almancil 8100 Loulé.
Tel: 089 97411/95156   Fax: 089 97295.
Alan Jarvis Esq.

Valmet-Loule, Valmet (Portugal) Gestão e Consultadoria Lda, Avenida José da Costa, 34, Bloco C, 2Dt2, Apt.201, 8100 Loulé.
Tel: 089 64886   Fax: 089 63637

Legal Services

David Sampson & Co., EN 125, Almancil, 8100 Loulé. Tel: 089 95556/95710   Fax: 089 97295
Telex: 58996 DSILAW P.

Predio de Sancho, Carvoeiro, 8400 Lagoa
Tel: 082 57623   Telex: 56768 LEGALS P.

MOVING...
to or from Portugal?

Gauntlett have weekly services U.K. - Algarve - U.K.
Regular internal services throughout Portugal.
Services to all European countries
and worldwide services by sea and air.

Gauntlett have warehouse storage facilities
in Portimão.
Packaging and unpacking facilities.
Customs clearing services.

ALGARVE OFFICE: Gauntlett International Transportes, Lda.
Estrada Nacional 125, 8400 Lagoa.
Tel: (082) 52047/52089/52551 - Telex 57429 GILDA P.

U.K. OFFICE: Gauntlett International Removals, Lda.
13 Farncombe Street, Godalming, Surrey.
Tel: (STD. 04868) 7766/28982/28983
Telex 859462 GIRL G

algrafica

GAUNTLETT International

Rua Nova da Alfarrobeira 8-1b, 2750 Cascais.
Tel: 01 284 0085   Telex: 12943 MOORE P
Fax: 1 284 4814/3246.

Dr. Rui Avelar, Rua João da Cruz, Portimão.
Tel: 082 26162.

Dr. Conceição Silva, Rua Conselheiro J. Machado,
73-1, Lagos.
Tel: 082 60420.

Dr. Fernando Pimenta Almeida Borges, Rua das
Portas de Portugal, 7-1c, Apt. 128-8602 Lagos. Tel:
082 60450.

Dr. Fernando José Tomé Carneiro, Rua Sotto
Mayor, 7-60e 8000, Faro.
Tel: 089 24036   Telex: 56189 SHADOW P.

Drs. Alvaro Correia Pina & Amadeu Carrilho,
Largo Dr. Antonio da Luz Silva, Lagoa.
Tel: 082 52877/52626.

Dra. Aldina Marum Diogo, Praca Alexandre
Herculano, 29r-c, 8000 Faro.
Tel: 089 21367.

Dr. Luis Galvão, Rua de Santo Antonio, 68-2o. Dto.
Faro.
Tel: 089 23099.

Dr. Carlos Gracias, Rua Ernesto Cabrita, 35,
Portimão.
Tel: 082 22630.

Dr. Olimpio Guerreiro, Portimão.
Tel: 082 63304   Telex: 56435

Dr. Maximiamo F. Nery, Rua Conselheiro Bivar,
10-1, DT, 8000 Faro.
Tel: 089 27119

Dr. Rui Dias, Largo Alves Rocades, Lagoa.
Tel: 082 52218.

Dr Paolo Alexandre de Pina, Dra Maria Isabel Pina,
Rua Dom Paio Pires Correia, 31-1o, Loulé.

Dr. Fernando Cabrita, Dr Fernando Anastacio,
Avenida de Liberdade, Edificio Brisa, 2a, Dt,
Albufeira.
Tel: 089 55447/54628.   Telex: 56237 LIBERA P.

Dra. Maria Teresa Silva, Dr. José Bulha, Dr.
Bernardino Duarte, Sociedade de Advogados, Rua
Antonio Alexio, Lt 28 Apartado 142, 8200
Albufeira.
Tel: 089 54975/55797/52255.   Telex: 56246
SULLEX P.   Fax: 54438.

Accountants

Deloitte Haskins & Sells, P O Box 198, Hillgate
House, 26 Old Bailey, London EC4M 7PL.
Tel: 01 248 3913 (R Chovill).

In Portugal:
D H & S, Avenida Eng. Duarte Pacheco Emp
Amoreiras-Torre 1-12 1000 Lisbon.
Tel: 01 693919/685626   Telex: 64429
Fax: 659322.

Arthur Anderson & Co., 1 Surrey Street, London
WC2R 2PS.
Tel: 01 480 7766 (Mrs S. E. Oakes.) -
Also have office in Lisbon.

Banks

Banco Espirito Santo e Commercial de Lisboa, 4
Fenchurch Street, London EC3M 3AT
Tel: 01 283 5381.

Banco Totto & Acores, 68 Cannon Street, London
EC4N 6AQ.
Tel: 01 236 1515.

Banco Português do Atlantico, 77 Gracechurch
Street, London EC3V OBQ
Tel: 01 865 6296.

All have branches in the main towns of the
Algarve.

Removal Companies

Gauntlett International, 13 Farcombe Street,
Godalming, Surrey GU7 3BA.
Tel: 04868 28982/3.

Robert Darvall Ltd., Acre Road, Reading. Berks
RG2 OSX.
Tel: 0734 86422.

SATELLITE TELEVISION

LAZER

THE PROFESSIONALS

LAZER VISÃO ANTENAS, LDA
Quatro Estradas, E.N. 125,
Almansil, 8100 LOULÉ
Tel: 089–97842/224/866 Fax: 089–97377

Satellite Television

In the last few years developments in this field have made major advances and it is now possible to receive a variety of television channels from the UK, France, Germany, Italy and the USA. Only a few companies have set up sophisticated operations with the latest equipment and technical backup. A company in the forefront of this technology is:

Lazer Visão Antenas Lda.
Quatro Estradas EN 125, Almancil, 8100 Loulé.
Tel: 089 97842/224   Fax: 098 97377

This company has considerable experience on installations of satellite and cable networks of all sizes for villas, apartments, hotels, and clubs – however large or small.
Equipment of the best quality is used and highly trained technicians have specialist knowledge of the reception and environmental problems particular to the Algarve.

The range of channels available is growing and currently includes BBC1 & 2, Sky, C.N.N., Super. Installations have been made at the Four Seasons Country Club and Fairways, Vilar do Golf, the Bovis Lakeside development, all at Quinta do Lago and Clube Barrington at Vale do Lobo.

Estate Agents (Government Licensed)

As mentioned earlier in this book, under Part II, it is highly recommended to deal only with Government Licensed Agents. The following is a list of some firms with names only, as all advertise extensively in local publications and addresses and telephone numbers can be obtained from these magazines, from directories or from tourist offices. The list runs roughly east to west:

Chalivillas
J. M. Sacurada
Selecção Imobiliaria
Sotavento

Brian Stephens Lda
Vilas & Homes
Jim Player
Jogn Barbara Real Estate Realti S.A.
John Hammond
Urbinvest
Vendavilla-Villagent Lda
Villalgarve
Helena Fernandes Lda
Lindahl
Joan Browne
Loja M
Continental Holmes
Algarve International
Iberus
Jan Frederick Luijt
John Evans - Real Sol Lda
Leanard D Morgan
Sargent and Sargent
Tanfield
Griffiths & Griffiths
Sadler and Moreira

Bibliography

Books of interest for further reading:
Buying Property in Portugal - an informative booklet published by the Portuguese Chamber of Commerce and Industry.
Living in Portugal by Susan Thackeray, Robert Hale.
The Algarve by José Victor Adragão (New Guides to Portugal), Editorial Prescença Lda.
Tourist Guidebook to Faro by Thomas Ribas.
Visitors Guide to the Churches of Faro by José Antonio Pinheiro e Rosa.
Algarve Guide to Walks by M B Condessa, Jorge Silva, José Garrido.
(All three above are available from Algarve Tourist Region Offices)
Timesharing - The Practical Guide by Brian Waites, David and Charles.

**C. C. DECORAÇÕES de
COSTA & CONTREIRAS LDA.**

Sítio de Escanxinas
Estrada de Vale do Lobo
Almancil – 8100 LOULÉ
Algarve, Portugal
Fax No. (089) 96906
Tel. No. (089) 96505

Moving to Portugal?

Here's a unique opportunity

Taxation legislation is changing all the time and becoming more and more complex. For instance Capital Gains Tax has just been introduced. Without up to date, professional advice, many expatriates pay out more - much more - than they need. Some even become the victims of double taxation, paying tax in two countries on the same portion of their income or assets. Unfair? Of course. And unnecessary.

A move to Portugal gives you a unique opportunity to devise a financial strategy that will effect significant tax savings for yourself and your family whilst also protecting your assets for your heirs. Some of the procedures need to be implemented before, not after, you buy a property here.

Prior to looking at houses or talking to architects and builders, you would do well to have a friendly, confidential chat with our staff. They will not only tell you of ways to mitigate your tax liabilities, but can advise on all aspects of your personal financial planning and help withmortgages for some specific developments.

The Riggs Valmet group of companies can trace its history to 1836 and is proud of its long international heritage. It together with its parent company Riggs National Bank of Washington, D.C. have offices in Switzerland, Hong Kong, Gibraltar, Spain, England, Washington, Miami and Nassau.

The Riggs Valmet office in Loulé, Algarve, can be a very real help to all nationalities moving to Portugal. Just phone (089) 64886 for a free confidential first appointment.

Consult the Friendly Professionals

Riggs Valmet at Loulé
A L G A R V E

Riggs Valmet (Portugal) Gestão e Consultadoria LDA. - Avenida José da Costa Mealha, Nº 34, Bloco C, 2 Dtº., Apt. 201, 8100 Loulé, Algarve, Portugal. Telephone: 089/64886, Fax: 089/63637

ATELIER DO SUL 3459

Visit our unique showrooms for a fabulous selection of fabrics,
furnishings and all the essential items for a beautiful home.
Come and take our professional advice and benefit from our
first class personal service whether you require just a table
lamp, a 3-piece suite or the complete furnishing of your
apartment, villa or development.
House packs at competitive prices.
Goodchilds also offer an excellent villa management service.

Call at our showroom now
For free Quotation
or send for our brochure
and further information, To:-

25, Rua D. João II - Mexilhoeira da
Carregação 8400 Lagoa - Algarve
Phone (082) 23202
Telex 58861 GOODSL P

Some Useful Portuguese Words and Phrases

Good morning/day	Bom dia
Good afternoon	Boa tarde
Good evening/night	Boa noite
Yes, no	Sim, não
Please	Faz favor
Thank you	Obrigado
I do not understand	Não compreendo
What does it cost?	Quanto custa
The bill please	Faz favor, a conta.
Where is....?	Onde é

Days of the week

Sunday	Domingo
Monday	Segunda-feira
Tuesday	Terça-feira
Wednesday	Quarta-feira
Thursday	Quinta-feira
Friday	Sexta-feira
Saturday	Sábado
Day	Dia
Holiday, feast day	Dia de festa
Post Office	Correio
Letter (express)	Carta (urgente)
Stamp	Selo

Geographical and topographical words

Water (carbonated)	Água (com gaz)
Avenue	Avenida
Glazed tiles	Azulejos
Boat	Barco
Dam, reservoir	Barragen
Town Hall	Camara Municipal
House	Casa
City, town	Cidade
Hill	Colina
Station (railway)	Estação
Road	Estrada
Lighthouse	Farol
Wood	Floresta
Cave	Gruta
Church	Igreja
Island	Ilha
Garden	Jardim
Square	Largo
Mountain	Montanha
Hill	Monte
(Town) wall	Muralha
Pinewood	Pinhal
Well	Poço
Bridge	Ponte
Door, town gate	Porta
State run hotel	Pousada
Square	Praça
Beach	Praia
Farm, Manorhouse	Quinta
Estuary, inlet	Ria
Street	Rua
Room, hall	Sala
Cathedral	Se
Mountain/hill range	Serra
Tower	Tower
Lane or alley	Travessa

Food guide

Poultry and meat	
Chicken	Frango
Rabbit	Coelho
Duck	Pato
Turkey	Peru
Lamb	Carneiro
Steak (various)	Bife
Kid	Cabrito
Ham	Fiambre
Pork	Porco
Beef	Vaca
Veal	Vitela
Fruit	
Apricots	Alperces
Almonds	Amendoas
Pineapple	Ananás
Nuts	Auelã
Raspberries	Framboesas
Orange	Laranja
Lemon	Limão
Apple	Maçã
Melon	Melão
Strawberries	Morangos
Peach	Pessego

Grapefruit	Toranja	Eggs	Ovos
Grapes	Uvas		
		Fish	
Vegetables		Tuna	Atum
Rice	Arroz	Cod	Bacalhau
Potatoes	Batatas	Sole	Linguado
Onions	Cebolas	Bream	Pargo
Carrots	Cenouras	Sword fish	Peixe-espada
Mushrooms	Cogumelos	Hake	Pascáda
Cabbage	Couve	Plaice	Pregado
Peas	Ervilhas	Bass	Robalo
Spinach	Espinafres	Red Mullet	Salmonete
Beans	Feijão	Salmon	Salmão
Peppers	Pimentos	Trout	Truta
Parsley	Salsa		

Plans and designs
An ultra modern villa or traditional style farmhouse. After one meeting with our architect, clients go home with plans and three-dimensional sketches of their villa. A unique service.

Restoration
We have been restoring old farmhouses in the Algarve since 1978, and have gained a reputation for our ability to turn a pile of stones into a comfortable, well-appointed home.

Building
We create well-construc ted custom-built homes to the highest standards, using the latest building methods and finest materials available.

A Complete Service
From finding a plot, organising legal requirements, building your villa and pool and landscaping the garden, through to arranging villa management and maintenance.

For more information on building, house design, land purchase and renovations, contact:

GOODFELLOW SMITH LDA
BUILDING CONTRACTORS
HOUSE DESIGNERS · RENOVATORS

Goodfellow Smith Lda., Apt. 240, Correio Central, 8000 Faro, Algarve.
Tel: Faro (089) 90166 Telex: 56771 MEDRON-P

HOTFOOT IT

TO
QUINTA DO LAGO

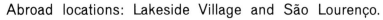

If the idea of buying property in the Algarve has crossed your mind, may we suggest that a quick visit to Quinta do Lago could prove highly profitable.

This lush and picturesque area, set amid 1,600 acres of pine forest, literally basks in the warm Algarvian sun.

In front of you is the Atlantic and miles of sandy beach. Close by are the waters of the Ria Formosa, a recognised nature reserve. And, right in the heart of it all, are two prime Bovis Abroad locations: Lakeside Village and São Lourenço.

LAKESIDE VILLAGE overlooks a calm lake and is surrounded by landscaped gardens, streams and bougainvillaea. Nearby is a superb 27-hole golf course (home of the Portuguese Open).

SÃO LOURENÇO is situated a little higher up on a beautiful wooded hillside. And for the keen golfer,